In Belfast by the Sea

CLASSICS OF IRISH HISTORY
General Editor: Tom Garvin

Original publication dates of reprinted titles are given in brackets

In Belfast by the Sea

✳

FRANK FRANKFORT MOORE

edited by Patrick Maume

UNIVERSITY COLLEGE DUBLIN PRESS

Preas Choláiste Ollscoile Bhaile Átha Cliath

First published in instalments in the *Belfast Telegraph*, 1923–4
First book publication, published by University College Dublin Press, 2007

Introduction © Patrick Maume, 2007

ISBN 978-1-904558-86-6
ISSN 1393-6883

University College Dublin Press
Newman House, 86 St Stephen's Green
Dublin 2, Ireland
www.ucdpress.ie

Cataloguing in Publication data available from
the British Library

Typeset in Ireland in Ehrhardt by Elaine Burberry
Text design by Lyn Davies, Frome, Somerset, England
Printed in England on acid-free paper by Athenæum Press

CONTENTS

INTRODUCTION

Patrick Maume

BIOGRAPHICAL NOTE[1]

Frank Frankfort Moore was born in Limerick on 15 May 1855 but grew up in Belfast, where his father established a successful business as clockmaker and jeweller. His upbringing was prosperous (*In Belfast by the Sea* describes memories of his youthful life in Bangor, still a village but about to become a suburb) and in some respects cultured (both French and German were spoken at home, and Moore received a fine literary education at the Royal Belfast Academical Institution, as well as studying with a private tutor in Portadown in 1869) but also restrictive.[2] The elder Moore was a member of the ultra-puritan Brethren sect, who forbade his children to read most forms of fiction except some religious and didactic titles, and taught his children to speculate on Biblical prophecy before they could read.

Moore's childhood was dominated by the conviction that the world was about to end. Regular visitors to the Moore household included the evangelist Michael Baxter, who identified Napoleon III as the Beast in the Book of Revelation; after the Emperor's deposition and death Baxter turned to identifying other potential Antichrists without loss of confidence in his ability to identify the

Final Enemy. Moore recalled the circulation of some verses entitled 'Mr. Baxter and the Beast', 'proving' that Baxter himself was Antichrist.[3] At the age of 15 the young Moore was soundly chastised by his father for telling Jerry Meneely, one of the celebrated working-class convert-evangelists of the Ulster Revival who assumed superiority to the young Moore because he had found salvation, 'to learn English instead of the argot of County Antrim before he posed as a preacher before educated people'.[4] Harsh Ulster fathers who turn their sons into hypocrites recur in Moore's work: this may be the origin of his lifelong habit of coining equivocally worded compliments which on closer inspection become insults.

The young Moore developed literary ambitions; as a teenager he published a book of Shelleyan sonnets, and exchanged literary ideas with a local poet and contemporary, Samuel Kennedy Cowan (possibly son of the Liberal Unionist Sir Edward Cowan, who was mayor of Belfast for two years in the early 1880s). One obituarist claims Moore went to sea for a time as supercargo on a windjammer. Between 1876 and 1892 he worked for the *Belfast Newsletter*, where he built up a remarkable record of travelling for a staff-member on a provincial paper, albeit combined with reporting for London papers; he reported on the 1878 Berlin Conference, travelled to South Africa to cover the 1879 Zulu War, and spent some time in the West Indies and South America. He also served as the *Newsletter*'s musical and dramatic critic, and eventually rose to become its deputy editor. He loved to hint that as a journalist he had acquired many unpublished and unpublishable local secrets, and knew all too well the difference between Belfast's self-righteous self-image and the reality.

Moore reacted against his background by developing an urbanely but decisively secular outlook (though he appreciated eloquent preachers as a form of entertainment) and by cultivating a dandyish persona – 'the dapper little figure with a mop of hair prematurely white; a downy moustache, which he was constantly caressing, and bright eyes, which he was as constantly snapping'. He welcomed John Tyndall's 1874 declaration of scientific naturalism at the 1874 British Association conference in Belfast, and observed with cynical humour the subsequent accommodations of the churches with Darwinism. Ironically, the Conservative *Newsletter* prided itself on its role as a defender of Protestantism; it was known to refer to the Liberal – subsequently Liberal Unionist – *Northern Whig* as 'our infidel contemporary' because the *Whig* was owned by the Unitarian Finlay family. The English-born *Whig* editor, Thomas MacKnight (1829–99; lived in Belfast from 1866) – a committed Anglican – was the other major journalistic memoirist of late Victorian Belfast; his Burkean moralism forms an interesting contrast with Moore.[5] Moore developed a personal cult of the eighteenth century, with a particular fondness for Oliver Goldsmith. His 1908 life of Goldsmith characteristically theorises that the writer's supposed simplicity masked a veiled wit comprehended by Johnson, though not by Boswell.

Moore contributed to London magazines and took to writing popular novels, many, with characteristic cynicism, for the Society for Promoting Christian Knowledge. Moore's first marriage to Grace Balcombe of Clontarf gave him access to London literary circles through Bram Stoker (who married Grace's sister Florence); Stoker's role as Henry Irving's manager encouraged Moore in writing zealous reviews of Irving's visits to Belfast and in denigrating the showier gestures of the well-established Barry Sullivan, darling of the poorer crowds in the theatre galleries. Moore's attacks on Sullivan were so vitriolic that at one point the *Newsletter* management ordered him to hand over reviews of Sullivan's latest productions to a junior reporter, whom he advised contemptuously to 'pour on plenty of butter and you will be all right'.[6] *In Belfast by the Sea* qualifies this slightly; while treating Sullivan as largely absurd Moore suggests that some Shakespearean roles – such as Othello – are better suited to Sullivan's broad-brush style than to Irving's psychological approach. Moore gives a vivid description of Irving performing at a charity recital in the Ulster Hall, and provides new insight into the relations between the great actor and his early producers, the Bateman family.

On at least one occasion Moore's savage criticism of a local Shakespearean production led to a libel action, in which the plaintiff won damages by emphasising Moore's reputation for verbal savagery; the case aroused so much interest that the next Belfast Christmas pantomime featured a comedian made up as 'Moore, the Man with the Caustic Pen'.

This journalistic vitriol reflected a sense of entrapment among provincial philistines. Moore increasingly longed to move to London and become a professional man of letters, but was deterred by the limited success of his early novels and the failure of his plays to establish themselves on the London stage. He experienced dismay on reading George Gissing's *New Grub Street*, with its picture of shabby London writers driven to sacrifice their talents in ceaseless brain-sapping hackwork. The success of his 1893 novel *I Forbid the Banns*, which eventually sold over 500,000 copies, led him to take the plunge. Moore celebrated liberation from Belfast by publishing in 1894 a collection of anecdotal reminiscences, *A Journalist's Notebook*, which gave widespread offence to his former colleagues by presenting Irish journalism as populated by mercenary opportunists. In London he met with rapid success, turning out a regular stream of popular novels, of which the most successful was *The Jessamy Bride* (1897), depicting the love story of Richard Brinsley Sheridan and his wife Elizabeth Linley. In all he published 66 novels, written with fluency and pleasure though without revision. 'The characters of his many novels are mostly flashlight photographs, mental or actual' commented a Belfast journalistic contemporary in an obituary which echoed its subject's brand of faint praise. 'It would be difficult to point to one which has an outstanding and compelling individuality'. He was a director of the Authors' Club and active in numerous other literary societies.

After Grace's death in 1901 Moore married Dorothea Hatton; they had three daughters. In 1904 Moore moved to Lewes in Sussex where he cultivated a formal eighteenth-century garden and continued his collecting activities; in 1922 he moved again to St Leonards (on the English south coast), also in Sussex. He died in St Leonards on 11 May 1931.

IN BELFAST BY THE SEA

In Belfast by the Sea appeared in 61 instalments in the *Belfast Telegraph* between September 1923 and June 1924. It was inspired by a visit to Belfast in 1921, and is loosely structured around an itinerary through his old haunts. The prologue describes memories of Bangor and Belfast Lough; after landing at the Custom House steps the central section tours central Belfast recalling the shops, residents and municipal buildings of Moore's youth. The last episodes discuss the theatrical and musical world of Belfast in the 1870s and 1880 and Moore's memories of the Royal Belfast Academical Institution (RBAI). The present text comprises about 60 per cent of the original 100,000 words; the abridgment aims at preserving the maximum amount of original material even where this means chopping out sentences and paragraphs, rather than a 'clean cut', preserving some sections complete while sacrificing others entirely.

This was not Moore's first literary exploration of Ulster since his departure in 1893. Moore was a consistent Unionist; while he had a certain fondness for the Dublin literati as charming and the peasantry he encountered while cruising the Shannon as dignified and generous, he saw them as socially inferior and politically incompetent. There had been a few Catholic pupils at the RBAI in Moore's time, but he felt the founders' insistence on mixed education had proved counter-productive. The Protestant pupils ignored their Catholic confrères except to ask which idols they were worshipping, whether holy water stung like acid, and similar questions.[7] The only Belfast Catholics Moore encountered socially were the furniture-dealers of Smithfield; during the debates on the first Home Rule Bill he experienced their indiscreet comments about what they would do when Home Rule gave them their turn on top. For all his reservations about Belfast provincialism, he admired its work ethic, which he himself exemplified in his relentless literary production. In the early 1880s he was briefly involved in a Belfast antiquarian society which attempted to promote Gaelic literature, but rapidly endorsed the view – expressed by most of those whom he canvassed to support the society – that reviving the Irish language could only hinder economic progress.

Moore reported on the Parnell Commission for the *Newsletter*, and saw the evidence laid before it about agrarian violence and seditious speeches as irrefutable proof of nationalist untrustworthiness. During the struggle over the Second Home Rule Bill he published three anonymous satires from a mildly disreputable Belfast local publisher. *The Diary of an Irish Cabinet Minister* (1892) [as by 'Phineas O'Flannigan'], *The Viceroy Muldoon: His Court and Courtship* (1892), and *Larry O'Lannigan JP: His Rise and Fall* (1893) portray nationalist politicians as corrupt and incompetent stage-Irishmen and ridicule Gladstone's Home Rule moralism as political opportunism.

During the 1912–14 Ulster Crisis Moore capitalised on public interest in the subject to produce a novel, *The Ulsterman*, and a travel-book, *The Truth About Ulster*.[8] These are generally pro-

Unionist, but their tone differs noticeably from *In Belfast by the Sea*; while the later work recycles some material from *The Truth About Ulster*, Moore omits such concerns of the earlier book as the Ulster businessman's skill in insurance fraud, the savagery of Ulster paternal discipline, the prevalence of whiskey-drinking, or the Belfast Presbyterian minister (notable for his denunciations of theatrical entertainments as leading to the Pit) whom Moore encountered in a London musical establishment 'in which the dresses of the whole corps de ballet might have been amply provided for out of the covering of the pulpit cushion [of his own church]'.

To some extent this reflects the fact that Moore is writing for a Belfast audience, though it may also be the case that the intervening world war and Irish conflict made the city of Moore's youth more attractive as it grew more remote. The Belfast audience also gives Moore's recollections a degree of intimacy, since he is appealing to shared memories. In some places this is troublesome, since Moore expects a passing reference or name to be familiar to his audience. Many such references have been edited out of this abridgement. In general, however, Moore is far enough removed from the events he describes to describe them without taking them for granted, and much of the interest of the series lies in his retrospective awareness of the magnitude of the changes he had witnessed: the last appearance of the old stagecoach and growing confidence in the railway (though at first a stage-coach guard perched uneasily on the carriage roof to reassure the respectable that this new machine was just as acceptable as the old coaches); the transition from the delivery of Cromac spring water house-to-house from a water-cart for those old-fashioned enough to distrust piped water, to the creation of a new water supply for the city from the Mourne Mountains; the development of public parks such as the Botanic Gardens under the supervision of such figures as the town clerk Sir Samuel Black and the talented botanist Charles M'Kimm; the first appearance of

Dunlop's pneumatic tyre at a Belfast bicycle-race (where it was greeted with laughter until it won); the shifting of the city's main axis of development from the east–west line of High Street to the broad new north–south axis of Royal Avenue, driven through the slums of Hercules Place; the move from a relatively restricted city centre where most shopkeepers lived over their premises to the development of a specialist commercial zone as professionals and businessmen shifted their residences to the growing suburbs along the Malone and Antrim Roads. One trend whose full significance he fails to notice is the role of the 'panorama' – a circular painting displayed on a cylindrical surface and viewed from inside – and its successor the diorama, a partly three-dimensional rotating display employing lighting effects as well as mile-long paintings displayed between rollers in a room-sized theatre, as precursors of the motion picture. Moore's references to these artforms shows that he despised both the diorama and its cinematic successor as insufferably vulgar; he refers to the wildly popular dioramas of *Ireland– Its Scenery, Music and Antiquities* and *Ireland: Its Shade and Sunshine* displayed at regular intervals by the Belfast surgeon T. C. Corry at frequent intervals between 1864 and 1888, only to mock their romanticised vision of Irishness.[9]

Most accounts of nineteenth-century Belfast emphasise the industrial development on which its wealth and confidence were based, and the bitter sectarian divisions which segregated the working-class residential areas. Although Moore discusses these in *The Truth About Ulster*, *In Belfast by the Sea* presents a bourgeois city – a site of consumption. Moore actively resists the idea of structuring his narrative around biographical self-revelation; instead, the audience sees Belfast through his eyes as he saunters in memory through the city centre gazing into the shops and reminiscing about their owners. This is a flâneur's Belfast; and implicit in it is a self-portrayal as sophisticated man of culture, taking a leisurely and unhurried stroll through familiar surroundings and presenting each thing of beauty or humorous anecdote as Moore collected, polished and presented his beloved eighteenth-century items of furniture and objets d'art. The downside of this self-conscious detachment is a fear of being overwhelmed or absorbed by the forces of unreflecting provincialism; this is at its most virulent in the hysterical racism with which he describes his visit to Robben Island, and shades into the mixture of social snobbery and genuine awareness of intellectual superiority with which he regards lower-class Catholics and undereducated evangelicals. (Racism and snobbery blend in *The Truth About Ulster*'s comparison of the Ulster revival to outbreaks of sexualised mass hysteria among West Indian blacks.) Moore's Belfast is not the whole story, and its omissions are damaging; but it does preserve aspects of the urban experience, too easily overshadowed by recurring political troubles.

A final purpose of *In Belfast By the Sea* is the defence of the cultural credentials of Victorian Belfast against Dublin's claims as a cultural centre (most acidly exemplified in his remark that while he would gladly sign a petition to have the Hugh Lane Bequest of modern paintings sent to Belfast, he saw no reason why it should go to Dublin to provide bonfire material in the next insurgency). Where *The Truth about Ulster* emphasises cultural provincialism and restriction, *In Belfast by the Sea* lovingly locates the city amidst the networks of late Victorian cultural endeavour: the slow growth of a local market for fine-art prints and engravings, the artists employed by the great publishing firm of Marcus Ward, the provincial tours of actors like Sullivan and Irving, the rise and fall of local music societies and their imported impresarios. An amusing sidelight on cross-community relations comes in his description of the unobtrusive descent of Protestant music-lovers on the Passionist church in Ardoyne when visiting artistes from the travelling Carl Rosa opera company were singing in the choir at Mass. These may not be comparable in impact to the Irish Literary Revival centred in the southern capital, but they are not negligible; and Moore also brings to his readers' attention the extraordinary number of prominent contemporary scientists, such as the oceanographer Wyville Thompson, who came from or spent much of their careers in Belfast – even if, in most cases, their greatest achievements took place elsewhere. In some respects his recollections support the recent research of Dr Eileen Black, who argues that the extent of artistic activity in nineteenth-century Belfast has been underestimated by scholars who focus on the small number of original painters and sculptors based in the town while ignoring the wider ambience of commercial galleries, private collectors, and visiting art exhibitions.[10]

Moore wrote in the reflected afterglow of the confident growth of Victorian Belfast. The decades of economic decline which followed, the sectarianism and exploitation which dominated the smaller streets behind the broad facades and rising department stores celebrated by Moore, should not disguise the fact that the development of Ireland's only major nineteenth-century industrial city was a major achievement, and that Moore was right in declaring that those who did it 'played a worthy part in their day, and they should not be forgotten'.

In Belfast by the Sea

I

*In Old Belfast · Changes in the City · Growth of Queen's Island
Once the Only Local Park*

A couple of years ago . . . on the steamer on my way to Belfast, I said
to someone with whom I had been discussing the North West light-
ship and the intricacies of the navigation of Liverpool river, as the
sailors call the Mersey: 'I wouldn't take an offer of a hundred
pilot's fees to bring a vessel up to the landing stage at Liverpool, but
I would back myself to steer anything that floats from the entrance
to Belfast Lough up to the Donegall Quay' . . . Soon after we had
passed Greypoint, I found that mine was a vain boast. I felt in every
sense 'at sea'. Some of the landmarks that I had known long ago I
recognised without difficulty, but the old seamarks with which I
had been familiar forty years before had disappeared. The navigable channel had then been a zigzag, but now it seemed about
straight. The steamer was passing over the bank which I had once
tried to negotiate with a yacht's dinghey that I had rowed single-
handed from Bangor, and that had scraped the mud with its keel,
but the Liverpool steamer kept its course, though it was half tide
without a mishap . . . I seemed to have lost all my bearings and
it was only when I lifted my eyes unto the hills and saw the
Napoleonic profile of MacArt's Fort that I felt among old friends.
If the Cave Hill had played me false I should have felt as the old
skipper of a coasting schooner must have done when, owing to
some thick weather and a misprint in his Jefferson's Almanac, he

found himself alongside the Quay of Derry when he was bound
for Belfast. But there was the good old Cave Hill, with Divis in the
distance, and I felt like William Tell of the Elocution book, among
the crags and peaks of his native mountains. I could view with
composure the alteration and distortions of the Lagan littoral on
both sides as we moved to our moorings.

Twenty-five years had passed since I had been at the Belfast
quay, and that space of time had plainly been sufficient to allow
that beneficent octopus called Harland and Wolff to throw its
tentacles east and west until the whole of 'The Island' had become
absorbed and assimilated with 'The Yard'. The Queen's Island
had actually been an island in my young days, and the 'Slips' at the
eastern end were but two in number – quite insignificant incidents
in the landscape. We could see when passing in the Bangor boats,
the riveters at work upon the plates of the ships that were being
built, and count the strokes of the two hand-wielded hammers as
they came down upon the red-hot pinhead with which a hidden
boy plugged the holes in the plates.

In those days the Island was Belfast's only park. It was reached
by a ferry from the County Antrim side, the boats carrying twenty
passengers, and resembling floating buses, and the attractions of
the place included a bathing pond, properly walled in, and a large
lawn, with mounds and shrubberies (of a sort) and a replica in
miniature of the Crystal Palace . . . In the centre, under the dome,
there was a fountain surmounted by Neptune and his trident, and
at the base were . . . sea-horses and nymphs of the modest type that
had a legendary existence before mixed bathing was sanctioned[1] . . .
An attempt was made . . . to found a Zoological Garden, for I distinctly remember, having heard of the liking of the ostrich for a
hardware diet, tempting the specimen with which a beginning was
made, with a few toothsome twopenny nails, and being greatly
disappointed at its indignant rejection of these delicate morsels.

I am not prepared to say if it was the decay of the Queen's Island as a place of giddy resort that gave the 'Yard' its chance . . . but I cannot believe that the mudbank – created, I believe, by Dargan, the engineer, in straightening out the navigable channel – ever contained the elements of a permanent popularity, in spite of a sporadic fete or two, and I think a balloon ascent added to its attractions.[2] At any rate Harland and Wolff made its clutch upon the place, and the mudbank became a Mount Morgan of Belfast.[3] There were four slips on the eastern end when I was permitted to be on the deck of a five-thousand ton steamer when it was being launched; and, by a singular coincidence, that very ship was sunk at what I might call my doorstep in the English Channel years afterwards, and looking out from where I write these lines, I see the loom of the great headland off which the disaster took place.

But while the Queen's Island – I believe it was called Dargan's Island before the visit of Queen Victoria in 1848 – was still isolated, there was an embankment on the other side of the Channel and this was called 'Thompson's Bank'. It became a stimulating promenade in winter or rough weather, for it formed a sort of causeway between a wide range of reclaimed land on the North and the waters of a turbulent stretch of water on the South. More than 50 years have passed since the splendid enterprise of the Harbour Commissioners admitted the water once more into the reclaimed land and educated it to become the Dufferin Dock. It was an equally fine spirit that caused this Northern Coast of the Channel to emulate the industrial Southern, and the enormous skeleton towers which give one the impression of Mr H. G. Wells's machines of the Martians in *The War of the Worlds*, sprang up on the waste that became the Yard of Workman and Clark. I asked a fellow passenger what these airy structures really were, and he replied that they represented the Trustees for the Debenture Shareholders.[4]

These Martian towers tended still further to confuse my topography; but further up the river was plain sailing compared to my voyage from the Quay to my destination a few miles away . . . The chime of the Ballast Office clock, and the boom of the bell of the Albert Memorial struck familiar notes; but where was the Linen Hall? What was the imposing square through which I was being driven? Whither had the great double lawn, most familiar of all, in front of the Royal Academical Institution vanished? On I was borne through a road bordered with houses where I had last seen nurseries and green fields – side streets where I had left yellow sands – churches where I had left public houses – Cinema Palaces – students' hostels . . .

The car pulled up.

'Five shillings', said the driver.

Then I knew it was really Belfast I had come to. The car was one that I might have jolted on 40 years before, and the driver was looking me straight in the face . . .

'Ay, five shillings – that's what I'm tellin' ye'.

Yes, there was no change in the tone. I was in Belfast.

II

The Clan Macmahon • Jovial Frank of that Ilk
When Bangor Hibernated

I am anxious that these familiar chats of mine on old Belfast should not follow the usual literary tradition of biographers or autobiographers, which entails the introduction of a central figure, with circumstantial evidence as to his or her early education – if any. The art of Mr Samuel Smiles[5] I would venture to ignore, substituting for it the casual gleanings of a memory that may be described as a treasury of the trivial. . . . I found during that last voyage to which I referred in in my last article – from Garmoyle to the First Lock thereof – that every glimpse I had of sea or shore, of street or steeple, brought back to my mind the scenes and the people of which I had been pars parva [a small part] fifty years ago, occasionally verging on sixty years ago, and I should like to pursue the unmethodical course on the 'that reminds me' principle so long as I can . . .

I am prompted to refer at this moment to some of those ancient mariners with whom I was familiar in the latter sixties and the early seventies at Bangor. I recall a few of them passing Greypoint when last coming up the Lough in the Liverpool steamer. There were half-a dozen of these 'longshore men' always at hand about the hotel end of the pier, and while two or three of them were glum, silent and morose, as if they had shot an albatross and had cooked it without providing the apple sauce,[6] others were excessively garrulous.

Among the latter was a jovial old soul by name Frank MacMahon. I am sure that there is at least one right honourable member of the Cabinet of the Northern State[7] who will recall with me the finespun yarns of old Frank, when cleaning the fish we had hauled up by the dozen between Groomsport and the Gobbins. We had our spirit stove aboard one of Frank's half-decked smacks, and the fish were cooked before they were well out of the 'wather' . . .

In those days Bangor hibernated for six months of the year. Now and again, when I had occasion to pay a visit to Ballyholme in the winter I was the only passenger in the train on its return. I remember once I stopped to speak to a man at the entrance to the station when the train was ready to start for its fifty minutes' journey to Belfast. The solitary porter was leaning against the waiting-room door, looking aft, as I might say.

'Is he a-coming, Bob?' called out the engine-driver, leaning out from his brake wheel.

'Ay, he's at the door', replied the porter.

'Bid him hurry or we'll not wait', said the man on the engine. I have never felt so important since.

The whole train had been held up till I should arrive!

But in those days, even in summer, the last train to Bangor left Belfast at 7.30, and it was said that the refreshment room was daily in charge of a bailiff. I cannot doubt that the duty was a coveted one. The manager was a Scotsman named —, and he was possibly the rudest man in County Down. I remember in a law case in which his replies had rather oversped the mark for brusqueness, the counsel for the other side asked him what his profession really was.

'An engineer, I told you before', he rasped out.

'Not a civil engineer, I should say', commented the barrister dryly.

But I can remember the time when Holywood was the terminus of the system. It was assumed that no one ever wanted to go to Bangor except in the summer, and I don't believe that anyone ever did. Newtownards was the station on the Co. Down Railway to which anyone compelled to make a journey in the close season took a ticket, and thence one proceeded by car to Bangor. The opposite shore of the lough was much better provided for. Such a place as Bangor was at that time is one that some people have been in search of for years – a picturesque seaside village with no train service. But when the boats were put into commission in the summer Bangor woke up. Many antiquaries like myself have written about the ancient Bangor boat service . . . The *Hero* and its consort, the *Heroine*, were stout, flat-bottomed side-paddle vessels which could reel off ten knots in an emergency, but fortunately that emergency never came. To us schoolboys the news that the *Hero* had been sold 'to run the blockade' came like a bit of Captain Marryat's novels.[8] We had no notion what running the blockade meant, but the phrase had a fine breezy, not to say piratical flavour, and we easily pictured honest Captain Brown wearing a cutlass and a broad leather belt with a full size buccaneer's buckle ready to hold his own against all-comers. Had we not seen him single-handed collect the fares on a Saturday evening? . . .

III

Mainly About Bangor That Was • Door-Step Embroidery Gray's Mill With One Horse

Considering that some of the most treasured memories of my life radiate from Bangor, it cannot be expected that I should be willing to forego all further reference to a place so intimately associated with my young days. I am sure that the whole trend of my life was influenced by my association one way or the other with Bangor. Were I disposed to write an autobiography I should feel compelled to analyse the varying parts played by the sounds of a sea and the silence of a mountain in the development of such elements as give colour and individuality to one's life . . . If I were forced to express an opinion on so complex a subject, I should not hesitate to assign to a glance from 'a grey eye or so' a place at the head of all such influences.

. . . Bangor meant for a boy with a bundle of sonnets ready for publication all that Shelley had apostrophised – with the glance thrown in; and, although I have been in many parts of the earth, and have sailed on all oceans, and have inhaled the air of many climes, from 'the spicey breezes that blow soft o'er Ceylon's Isle'[9] to the miasmic breath of the Amazon banks, I confess that the first 'careless rapture' that Bangor brought me remains with me still. All my early friendships were centred there, and when I stood in the old churchyard two years ago I felt myself in the midst of old friends . . .

Great though the changes may be which one observes on coming to Belfast after an absence of twenty-five years, they are not so striking, possibly because they are not so concentrated, as those which have taken place in Bangor. A Liverpool man surveying the slopes of the little bay with me forty years ago, cried:–

'My word! What a place we would make of this if it was within reach of Liverpool!'

I knew that he had in his mind Southport and Blackpool.

. . . The old Bangor as we knew it has given place to what is only a lesser Southport. Of course, the old character of the place has been obliterated, but the curve of the little bay has not been altered, the stimulating breeze from the North-east still sends the waves hurrying shoreward from Ballymacormac to the Pickie, and I suppose that thousands enjoy the strenuous efforts of a brass band to vamp an obbligato to whatever the wild waves may be saying at the moment.[10] Old Bangor has been built out of existence, but new Bangor is a live place for a live community, and thousands of people have benefited by the transformation.

When I first made the acquaintance of Bangor there was only one house – a farm building – from Gray's Hill and past the Pickie Rock to Carnalea. The rocky slope had a bridle path along the ridge, and sheep cropped the herbage almost down to the water's edge. On the opposite shore there was the group of villas known as Seapoint; and in the course of time a more imposing row sprang up facing the road to Ballyholme; but there were not half-a-dozen villas between these and Glenghana, the dower-house of the Dufferins . . . In numbers of the cottages at the upper part of the Main Street there were hand-looms, and at all hours of the day a passer-by could hear the 'clackerty-clackerty', as it was called, of the weavers' looms.

When my head barely reached to the top of the half-door of one of these cottages I was accustomed to look into the room where the work was going on. I remember that there were two looms, back to back, and, blocking the entrance to the room beyond, a woman at the spinning-wheel, the purring sound of which made a background, so to speak, for the rhythmical 'clatter' of the flying shuttles and the rasping of the dry wood of the clumsy machines which produced linen that would last for a hundred years – the finest linen that was to be obtained in the world. In the long summer evenings, when the men were still weaving within, the girls used to sit on the door-step working at their embroidery – that tambour-flowering which they call cutwork. I am sure that one could find a hundred young men so occupied outside the cottages in the Main Street, Ballymagee Street, and the higher parts of Gray's Hill.

At the back of these streets there were garden strips growing potatoes, and there was no lack of sound here either, for every cottage had its pig or two – occasionally a goat. I seem, as I write these words, to see the steam that came from the big iron pot suspended over a turf fire for the cooking of the food for the pigs' evening meal. The mingling of the household smells in no way suggested the perfumes of Araby the Blest. The flax was damped for certain operations, and it was noisome; but it was like Rimmel's shop compared to the reek of the fields beyond, where, after being cut, the flax crop was rotting.[11] I have met people who professed to be able to enjoy a walk on a road bordered by the flax ditches, but . . . I never got used to it, and as a great deal of flax was grown

in the fields between Bangor and Conlig and Newtownards in one
direction, and between Groomsport, Donaghadee, and Millisle
in another, it can easily be believed that I found contact with fish
preferable to that with flax in the long evenings. I was in a boat all
my spare time. The sweet salt scent of the sea was then, as it has
always been since, a delight to me.

There was lacking in that little community no element that one
associates with a village colony of the past. It must never be
forgotten that Bangor was a colonial village as much as Boston ever
was. There was no trace of Irishry about it. The few Gaelic words
that were to be heard in the fields or along the coast came from the
North of Scotland, not from the South of Ireland. The inhabitants
had inherited all the traditions of work from their forefathers on
the other side of that strip of water – work and prayer. If they were
fully employed on weekdays . . . they were quite as busy on
Sundays. The church and the meeting-houses were attended with
a regularity that could not have been surpassed even at Plymouth
Rock . . . My recollections of old Bangor – the girls sitting with
their outwork round their doors, strolling barefoot and with a shawl
about their shoulders to the well off the Main Street or the pump
on the Church Road to wait their turn with their water cans – of
the elderly God-fearing heads of the household riding to
Newtownards Market Square with a bale of unbleached linen
behind them – differ very slightly from those set down in the early
chronicles of the colonists who made the sterile tracts of Maine to
blossom as the rose. They were animated by the same spirit as that
which turned Ulster from the most barren of Irish provinces to . . .
the most fruitful.

IV

Pews and Their Occupants More Than Forty Years Ago

Bangor Church about fifty years ago . . . was very different, so far as the interior was concerned, from what it was when I visited it two years ago. The alterations have to a certain extent changed its character, but it is not for me to suggest that the interior has been in any way spoiled. After all, a church does not exist as a museum of the inconsistencies and inconveniences of the past. Whatever of picturesqueness there was about the old three-decker pulpit and the square loose-boxes with high backs which were the old pews, was only interesting as a beaver hat or a crinoline is interesting – the obsolete has a certain charm . . . I was conscious of a little shock when I returned to Bangor Church after an interval of nearly forty years, and found that so much which I remembered had disappeared. But I found before I had walked to the end of the nave that . . . my memory was equal to restoring all that the new restoration had done away with, and I could easily imagine myself in the church as I had left it.

The original organ loft was really a loft. It was a lofty gallery just above the entrance to the church, and there was ample accommodation in front for those instrumentalists who, at the beginning of the nineteenth century, were 'on the strength' of every village church, with the servants of the 'gentry' behind. The Communion table was, of course, under the oriel window on the left; facing the window, was the raised 'reading-desk' – it was never called the lectern – and on the other side of the window was the pulpit. It was very little higher than the pews on the raised transept on the same side of the church, where the organ is at present placed. The pews on the corresponding part opposite were on the floor, and not elevated. Nearly all those in the body of the church were square roomy structures with doors, and seats on three sides so that one could sit with one's back to the 'business-end' – pardon the seeming irreverence – of the church, a position I confess I could never bring myself to assume. On each side of the entrance a few pews were of the more restricted pattern and in the aisle there were several unbacked free benches. Just below the reading-desk there was a very large square pew, with the rector's on the same pattern, below the pulpit. The construction differed in no respect from that of hundreds of village churches in England and Ireland, and the impression it produced was distinctly one of homeliness rather than austerity. On the walls on each side of the oriel were stone and slate tablets – one of them I recollect had reference to 'my Lorde Clandeboye', and it bore the date 1652, as far as I remember – it was certainly seventeenth century.

I failed to find this tablet on the walls when I looked for it two years ago. There were also some lettered slabs of great age on the floor; these doubtless marked the entrances to the vaults and are preserved in another part of the edifice.

My memory has no difficulty in discharging the duties of a sidesman in conducting many of the members of the old congregation to their seats in the church of more than forty years ago. The large front pew on the right hand side was that of the Lord of the Manor, Mr R. E. Ward. With his beautiful wife and daughter and the constant visitors to Bangor Castle, the distinction that attached to that pew was at all times very marked. I cannot remember who were the occupants of the seats immediately behind the manor pew, but one very large square one was held by a Mr M'Cullough and his sister. On the opposite side was the family of the Cleelands of Rathgael, the Nicholsons of Balloo, and, I think, the Sharman Crawfords, but I am nearly sure that Major Sharman Crawford, a handsome and genial old gentleman of a pronounced military type, sat at one side of the reading-desk, close to the family of Mr Foster Connor, who in 1869 built Sea Court. The front row nearest the pulpit on the raised transept was taken by the Cowan family, and a handsomer group could not be imagined . . . The front sitting on the opposite side was occupied by another handsome family, the Higginsons, of Carnalea House . . .

These are all the local people whose faces came before me when I stood at the door of renovated Bangor church; but with them there came vivid pictures of past summers when the church was crowded with the summer residents. Very different were the winter congregations. But the regular attendants were always courteous to the casuals. Seats were somehow forthcoming for all, even upon special occasions when more or less distinguished prea chers took part in the service. Among these were Dr Chadwick, and Dr Thresham Gregg[12] . . . I shall never forget the impressive way in which the former quoted Tennyson's lines, 'Too late –too late! Ye cannot enter now', nor have I ever heard the Decalogue declaimed . . . as it was by Dr Gregg. In those days the Rector was the Rev. Dr Binney, whose long connection with the church is suitably commemorated . . .

V

Startling Incident In Bangor Church
Rector and Sir D. Dixon • Drill Sergeant Methods
[Omitted]

VI

*Great Organist at Bangor Castle • Notable Names in Cricket
Both at Home and in Lord's*

Mr Robert Edward Ward, of Bangor Castle, always took an active
interest in music, and was himself an amateur of great intelligence,
his favourite instrument being the violoncello. He was for long
president of the Belfast Philharmonic Society, and I recollect his
playing a solo at one of their concerts in the Ulster Hall. The fine
hydraulic organ – one of the earliest set up in the North of Ireland
– which he put up in his large music-room at the castle, was early
played on by Sir Robert Stewart, the Professor of Music at Trinity
College, Dublin.[13] He was a frequent guest, with his beautiful
daughter, at the castle, and I shall not soon forget the effect which
his magnificent treatment of Handel's Largo had upon me when,
very late one night, I was passing through the grounds near the
castle. It was a very still night, and through the open door there
came such strains as were a revelation to me. Frequently though I
had heard the Largo interpreted by great organists, I felt on that
night that I was listening to it for the first time. And while I stood
entranced at the close a breeze sprang up, and suddenly all the
shrubberies awoke and the waving boughs and restless leaves gave
me the impression of nature's response – the woodland's recognition as of a living thing of the music that had broken the starlit
silence of that night. Sir Robert Stewart was one of the greatest
organists that ever lived, for not only was his technique at the
keyboards exceptional, but his intellectual grasp of the composer's
design was masterly. His playing of passages which he chose
upon one occasion in Dublin seemed to me to be inspired. I think
I remember at least three concerts conducted by him at Bangor

Castle . . . I also heard Lord Arthur Hill sing a solo in the same place.

Within the grounds of Bangor Castle we had our cricket field, and our Saturday matches were among the events (in our eyes at least) of the summer season. The Bangor team was got together by S. K. Cowan, who at his public school in Bromsgrove had a bowling reputation, which he maintained at the North of Ireland ground, where he took part for several years in first-class matches. Upon one occasion I know he played against an eleven of All England, which included the great W. G. Grace. Two of the Percival-Maxwells now and again played for Bangor, and among the earliest and certainly the most punctilious and business-like of the club was Henry Montgomery, who even in those days had his heart set on the ministry . . . The boy was father to the man in his case, and assuredly the high respect in which he was held by all who came in contact with him when emerging from his boyhood was not abated when the aim of his life was realised, and he occupied one of the most important pulpits in Belfast, and became Moderator of the General Assembly. Another member of the club who has attained a well-earned distinction was Mr H. M. Pollock, who came naturally into the position of Minister of Finance in the Northern Cabinet. I used to see a good deal of him during those early years in Bangor, and I know that when any new social movement was on foot in our little community his advice had to be sought; . . . he avoided any position of prominence, but he was ever a thoughtful worker, hard-headed, and far-seeing, and without prejudices . . .

VII

Kindly Curate and the 'Divil' • Story of a Testimonial
'Rosie' of Ballymagee Street

I should have it on my conscience if I were to close my reminiscences of old Bangor without a kindly word for good Dr Binney's
curate the Rev. Michael Beattie, for he had a kindly word for many,
spoken with all the mellowness of Mayo, with a garnish of Galway.
An interview with him was like turning over the pages of a Guide
to Connemara, with highly coloured illustrations, though I believe
he originally came from Fermanagh. Sometimes he failed to avoid
such a pitfall as yawns for an honest man over the inconsistencies
in the English pronunciation of such prayer book words as 'our
adversary the Devil', and the 'adversities' from which one hopes to
be delivered . . . He succeeded by the force of his personality in
overcoming the prejudices of no inconsiderable section of the
people who felt that an alien brogue concealed but indifferently an
adherence to Rome, and four saints' days a week.[14] The coast-folk,
who had always been distrustful of the soft slur of the Irish brogue,
accepted the Rev. Michael without feeling that he was a Father
Mickey in disguise.

During his first year in Bangor I made a tour through
Connemara, and at Clifden, where he had lived, I heard a good
deal about Mr Beattie, and all that I heard was in his favour. He had
been associated with the Church at Clifden, though he had not
attained to the rank of reverend until the Disestablishment, when
the Church doors were opened wider than they had ever been
before, and a University degree was not regarded as a 'sine qua
non' for ordination. I think that his first curacy was Bangor, and I
believe that his previous experience of the Atlantic coast enabled

him to give a hint or two about the management of a half-decked smack to the boatmen who had never known heavier seas than were to be encountered at the entrance to Belfast Lough. He came to Belfast after some years in Bangor and was curate at St Anne's when the Rev. Robert Hannay[15] was Vicar. Later he became a military chaplain, and was also in charge of the local branch of the Seamen's Mission. He invited me to join his party to the old train-ing ship, *Gibraltar*, for a service, and then down the Lough. We had three services in all on that Sunday and the same number of sermons, and Mr Beattie arrived in good time for evening prayer at St. Anne's. He gained confidence in himself as the years went by, and I actually saw him in the Strangers' Gallery in the House of Commons; but if he went there hoping to better his pronun-ciation of the English language, he might as well have stayed in Connaught . . . A Belfast merchant who had once occupied a high place in local society, and had patronised him pretty freely, applied to him to say a good word for his candidature for a humble secre-taryship in Dublin. 'Tell them that I have an uncle who is a baronet and a son in the Gordon Highlanders' was the gentleman's plea. 'I'll do nothing of the sort', said Mr Beattie. 'I'll only say that you know book-keeping and office work, and that I believe you to be a respectable man.' The gentleman got the post he coveted.[16]

I wonder if there is still living anyone who recollects one 'Rosie', who flourished exceedingly in a cottage at the bottom of Ballymagee Street, on the production of a delicacy known as 'Rosie's Lumps'. More than fifty years ago she occupied a high place in the affection of a community who had not yet succumbed to the blandishment of the highly decorated and beribboned chocolate box or the ener-vating refinement of the fondant glace. The available sweetmeats of those days were few in number. There was little choice left to us except in the colouring of the sugar candy, or the crispness of the Everton toffee . . . Some flamboyant tastes were catered for with bulls' eyes, or the brittle sugar-sticks with Venetian glass decorations, but beyond these the fastidious palate had to be content with what was known as fig-cake – a preparation of dried figs with almonds subjected to high pressure into the shape of a Scotch bannock . . .

VIII

Royal Ulster Club's Origin • Earliest Moving Spirits Great Co. Down Yachting Peer

. . . I cannot give all the information I would like respecting the inauguration of the Royal Ulster Yacht Club . . . [Perhaps] some fully-qualified member will undertake a complete history of its formation and progress . . . Such a chronicle would be of immense interest to yachtsmen all over the world. I have had experience, in many seas, of the influences of Bangor and Belfast Lough generally . . .

Just as a man brought up in Meath turns his thoughts towards the horses in the place of his emigration, so the Belfast man looks about for a boat. All along the Atlantic coast of North America, from Newport[17] down to the Keys of Florida, you will find yachts manned by the descendants of Belfast men and Larne men and Carrickfergus men. It is in the blood of the descendants of those sturdy Ayreshiremen, who, two hundred years ago, crossed the narrow channel . . . I have always cherished the hope that some day a picture would be painted by Arthur D. McCormick, one of the greatest marine artists alive,[18] illustrating the historic account that exists of the Sabbath visit of the boatful of Ayrshire Presbyterian farmers to the opposite coast when one of their favourite ministers, who had accepted a call from a congregation of their brethren on the Irish side, was to preach. For myself I have often pictured the return trip on the Sabbath afternoon, when one may be sure that the various doctrinal points of the sermon were actively discussed in the stern sheets of those undecked yawls with the big brown patched sails . . .

The Ulster Yacht Club was the natural outcome of the sailing traditions of Loch Ryan, the Clyde, and Belfast Lough . . . I remember when a couple of rooms in Bangor were sufficient for its requirements . . . I rather believe that the earliest moving spirits in its creation were James Moore, Arthur Hill Coates and Robert Workman . . . I heard the name of Charles M'Alister spoken of as one of the originators of the club. He lived at Holywood and there was quite a fleet of small yachts hailing from Holywood, Marino, Cultra and Craigavad . . . I am pretty sure that Mr Arthur Hill Coates was the first secretary . . . The debt that was due to him in his efforts to give the club a position worthy of being alongside the Royal St George's or the Clyde clubs could not be over-estimated. There was no one in the North who had the same influence. He was a fine organiser, and a scientific sailor as well. I remember his ten-ton cutter, the *Raven*, which he sailed with one deck hand only.

Another splendid handler of a boat of any rig was James Moore, who, to the great regret of anyone who ever knew him, died two years ago. He also was the kindest man who ever held a tiller . . . both in business and socially . . . Every year of our long friendship but increased my affection for him . . . Once when I was a visitor to the St George's Yacht Club,[19] the most notable of the southern yachtsmen of that day agreed that James Moore had no equal in southern Ireland . . . Dr Murney was another first-class sailor of the old days . . .

Among the greatest of all-round yachtsmen of the North,
however, was the first Marquis of Dufferin and Ava . . . the greatest
Ulsterman of the nineteenth century.[20] More than sixty years ago
his account of a yachting trip to Iceland was published under the
title of *Letters from High Latitudes*. It was one of the most
delightful of all yachting chronicles . . . Lord Dufferin took part in
a single-handed contest among yachtsmen of the Royal Ulster, and
showed himself to be a consummate hand at the tiller. But he was a
scientific navigator as well, and could work out his position with
the sextant and chronometer with any shipmaster holding the
'extra ticket'. At one time when he was about to take a long voyage,
he thought it might be well to brush up his navigation and he
obtained the services of the most competent teacher in Belfast –
one who had trained hundreds of shipmasters for 'passing the
Board'. This man told me afterwards that in the presence of his
lordship he felt like a cabin boy . . . Of the part played by his boat
during his difficult mission as plenipotentiary to Constantinople, I
heard much . . . My informant was one of the Embassy staff, and he
assured me that it was Lord Dufferin's studied neglect of the
Sultan and his scrupulous attention to his yacht that put the
negotiations on a footing to be appreciated by the procrastinators
of the Golden Horn.

. . . I received a long and interesting letter from him written from
his bed during his last illness . . . he sent me an autograph copy of
the poems of the mother whom he so revered, and another of his
Book of Helen's Tower,[21] inscribed by himself. A fortnight later I
landed from the mail steamer at Barbadoes, and the first cable
which I read on the board at Government House, told of the death
of this greatest of governors – supreme among those of Canada,
supreme among those of India.

IX

'Hesperus Becalmed off Black Head' · Story that Hinged on it Regatta Visitors of Seventies

. . . Early in the seventies two boats well known in the Lough were carrying all before them at regattas. The larger was the schooner *Egeria*, the owner of which was Mr John Mulholland, who at a later date became the first Lord Dunleath; the other was the cutter *Quickstep*, owned by a Mr Fulton. I forget what was the tonnage of the former, but I fancy it was far over the hundred, and I am certain that it won a first prize for every ton . . . Its feats were rehearsed week by week from school to school of the Royal Academical Institution, and by some boys whose names afterwards became well known among the world's greatest shipbuilders. Mr Mulholland's was quite a family boat, but I do not think he sailed it himself – certainly not at a regatta. Mr Fulton, however, was the designer of his *Quickstep*, and I believe the builder as well . . .

I daresay that the scores of cups won by the *Egeria* are among the heirlooms of the Dunleath family . . . An excellent lithograph of the famous schooner was published when it was at the height of its fame. It may be that in these days of speed it would run no chance when competing with the *Britannia* or Mrs Workman's beautiful cutter . . . but for a fine family racer, combining comfort with speed, and laying the emphasis upon the former, I am sure that Mr Mulholland's schooner had no equal in its time.

X

Early Recollections of S. K. Cowan • Happy Days at Glenghana
His Mastery of Greek Verse
[omitted]

XI

Absent-Minded Poet • His Parodies of Tennyson
Search for the River Shannon
[omitted]

XII

Wreck as Fishing Rendezvous • Two Drowned at Regatta
The Pilots' Lighthouse Home

Gradually working my way up the Lough to Belfast . . . I must be allowed a moment's delay at the Garmoyle lighthouse . . .

The old Garmoyle lighthouse was the commodious home of the Lough pilots, and I need hardly say that when I . . . [became] acquainted with the thrilling conditions under which they pursued their profession, I made up my mind to qualify for a pilot's certificate. The dormitory arrangements were enough to captivate any boy with a sea sense. The neat bunks were around the wall of the octagonal first floor . . . and upon stormy nights the spray breaking over the rocks at the foundation, dashed against the windows of this beautiful big room, and what more could anyone hope for in life than to lie awake in a cosy bunk and hear the roar of the gale and the crash of the breakers? When to these ideal conditions of life [was added] the occasional joy of a watch in the lamp-room ... reached by a narrow iron ladder, it seemed amazing to me that every man of spirit did not seek to be a pilot.

In my very young days the pilots had a stout cutter for their cruising about the entrance to the Lough, awaiting the vessels bound for the Belfast quays. But later, their boat was schooner-rigged ... now they have a motor launch ... The tin-kettle has triumphed, but at the sacrifice of much of the old picturesqueness ...

What ships I remember seeing under sail in the Lough or anchored off Carrick Roads! Big clippers from Baltimore, and emigrant-carrying barques taking passengers to the United States before the Californian gold craze had altogether passed away. I recollect very well seeing a great Nova Scotia barque warped into dock, the captain wearing a chimney-pot hat and a frock coat, as if he were going to church in Piccadilly. But then the cricketers played in tall hats, and the harbour police were so crowned.

In those old days one had a chance of hearing a seaman's 'chantey' before a ship had left the river; but you cannot imagine a 'chantey' sung with the obbligato of a donkey-winch. But once when on a trip to South America the Royal Mail steamer in which I sailed kept almost abreast, at a distance of a mile or two, of a magnificent steel five-masted ship with every stitch of canvas set. We exchanged signals, and our captain told me that she was one of the big sailing-vessels ... recently ... turned out of a Belfast yard ... he gave it as his opinion that there were no better seamen afloat than ... from the coasts of Antrim and Down.

It was when I had just emerged from an infant school that I was brought by my nurse, who had many maritime connections, and hoped to have still more, to witness the launch of a vessel from the old slip which I think belonged to the early shipbuilder named Ritchie ... [22] just beyond the Harbour Office and the dry dock of

Messrs MacLaine, who made a fortune by ship-repairing. The vessel was launched without ceremony – I think I would remember such an incident as the breaking of a bottle of champagne on the bows; I certainly do remember that the name painted on the stern was '*Queen of the East*'. Hundreds of people watched the launch, and there was a fine display of bunting . . . I suppose that the vessel was over two hundred tons . . . but what impressed me most deeply was the fact of the waters in the dock being covered with the timbers of the 'ways', whether by the tidal wave caused by the launch or by some accident I cannot say, but it seemed as if all the floating wood became the perquisite of the shipwrights, for within a few minutes scores of men, fully clothed, were swimming in every direction, eagerly collecting the timber, pushing it before them to the shore and carrying it off.

XIII

From Garmoyle to South Atlantic • Strange Meeting Place Isle of Lepers and Lunatics

Many years had passed since my first visit to old Garmoyle lighthouse . . . Robbin Island . . . was well worth a visit – not, however, a second. It is nothing more than a sandbank some miles long, lying off Table Bay. On a gorgeous day in January – mid-summer at the Cape – we set off in a small and very wheezy steamer from Capetown, within half a mile of the yellow sands of the beach we cast anchor. Although our steamer drew only six or seven feet of water, the 'shoaling' was so gradual that we could not with safety get any closer. A large flat-bottomed boat came along, and into this we transhipped; but even this craft grounded while still a hundred yards off the landing-place . . . half-a-dozen stalwart men . . . waded alongside our barge and we were expected to play pick-a-back with them if we had a mind to land! What added some degree of piquancy . . . was the broad arrow on the sleeves of the dirty white tunic which each of these men wore . . . I threw myself on the broad shoulders and upon the mercy of a smiling Hercules of this band, hoping to ensure my safe landing by slipping half-a-dozen cheroots under his cap. 'Thank you, sir', he whispered. 'I'd rather have smokes than tracts any day'. 'Tracts?' I said. 'Tracts – religious stuff; goody-goody to show the poor convict the error of his ways.' What are you here for?' I enquired. 'Killing a nigger, sir', he replied breezily. 'I've still a cheroot or two left, where can I stow them for you?' I said. I had had some months experience of niggers in South Africa, and I felt that I owed a whole box of cheroots to this man who had availed himself of . . . a treat which I had frequently promised myself.

We had not quite left the shallow beach . . . before we found ourselves surrounded by . . . lepers! The loathsome disease had left its mark upon all the poor wretches that approached us, and in a negro or a Malay its ravages are loathsome beyond expression. Some had their hands eaten away, and more than one had the appearance of a death's head where a face should have been . . . I made a rush inland, but escaped from one horror only to be confronted with another, for from the side of a long wooden shed there came a crowd of about a dozen gibbering figures of all ages – waving their arms, yelling like monkeys, and some praying like caricatures of a parson. This fascinating spot . . . was the abode of a community of convicts, lepers and lunatics deported from Cape Town . . .

In the distance there stood a majestic lighthouse, and I made for this landmark after a gesture of salutation to the horrors that had greeted me – a gesture that discouraged them from following me. The lighthouse stood up nobly surrounded by a properly spiked iron railing, with a padlocked gate, and standing at the door with his hands in his pockets, smoking a pipe, was a man whom I had last seen years before among the pilots at Garmoyle Lighthouse.

He had the regular Islandmagee face . . . He could not recognise me – I had only been a schoolboy when I made his acquaintance, and he was startled, but in the undemonstrative way of the Ulster coast man, when I . . . enquired if he was not Captain —. He would not compromise himself by replying on the spur of the moment. He looked at me from his doorway with half closed, cautious eyes. Then he removed his pipe, examined the bowl, rubbed it on his sleeve, and spat to one side . . . I could not help laughing, while he remained silent – still cautious. 'Look here', I said, 'after you clear the lighthouse at Garmoyle, is the course for The Maidens east by nor' or nor'-nor'-east?'

He did not smile, he knocked the ashes out of his pipe, and walking to the gate loosed the padlock, scrutinising my face all the time.

'I never seen you before', he said, with a shake of the head. 'You be to come in.'

Then my friend, who was wearing the tropical uniform of an officer of Sappers, came up, and the lighthouse man perceived the possibility of my visit having an official connection . . .

'You'll be coming inside, out of the hate, sir – it's quare an' hot the day', he remarked, quite cordially. 'It's not an inspection, sir?' he added, turning to the officer.

'Nothing of the sort, my man. Make your mind easy', replied the latter. 'I suppose this is about the only safe place in this infernal island.'

'Ay, when the gate's locked; but you'll come inside awhile. You be to hang on to the boat goes back to the Bay. Are ye there, Mary Ann?'

We entered his comfortable room on the ground floor, and Mary Ann appeared . . . with a tray and tumblers.

We chatted together on many topics – the island, the scandal of lunatics at large, the unfitness of lepers as congenial companions, and so forth. It was only when the man had manoeuvred me up to the lantern gallery that he asked me who I was. Then I found that he knew all about me, and he lost something of his previous reticence. He told me that he had signed on as first mate of a Glasgow barque bound for the River Plate, whence she had got a cargo for Port Elizabeth. A gale off Cape Agulhas had dismasted her, but the crew had been picked up by a Donald Currie steamer and brought to Cape Town, where he had come upon Mary Ann, whose father had sufficient influence . . . to give him the job at which I had found him.

He was at no time fluent in telling me his story. I only got it from him by snatches, and I got the impression that there might have been an episode or two in his life which he did not feel called on to reveal . . . I could not understand how any man would accept the post that he occupied . . . unless he had reasons of his own for at least a season of seclusion. Of course I did not hint to him in any way that I thought his choice of employment peculiar; we exchanged remarks about various people whose names were known in Belfast and Bangor, and he was certainly conversant with Whitehead. He told me that he had not got a master's ticket; he had meant to . . . try to pass the Board after his voyage to the River Plate: he 'disremembered' who was the superintendent at Belfast; and he had 'heard tell' that before Captain Spinner had left he would hardly pass anyone . . . Our chat was interrupted by the sound of my steamer's warning whistle, and I said good-bye . . .

'If you go back and see any of them chaps at Garmoyle you needn't let on to them that you seen me here', he said.

I assured him that it was extremely unlikely that I should ever [come] across any of his former associates . . .

'I used to think quare an' long when I first come here and minded Garmoyle; but now . . . ah, there's yer whistle. Ye be to hurry.'

I did hurry, but in a minute or two I glanced back.

He was still standing at the iron gate looking after me.[23]

XIV

Boats with Electric Names • A Burnsite's Experience
Shipowner Mixed Up With Poet

I have been trying to recall the names of the cross-Channel steamers of my young days, but I have not succeeded to any appreciable extent. Everyone of middle-age must have had some experience of the elusive nature of names and figures . . . There was a direct London line and a Rotterdam line, as well as a weekly service to Dublin, usually laden on the return trip with barrels of Guinness's stout. The Barrow line was started long after the Fleetwood. It early formed a connection with the Midland Railway of England. I re-collect seeing Mr Robert Henderson, the agent for the Fleetwood boats – a distinguished-looking old gentleman – in the latter 'sixties, and the father of beautiful daughters, one of whom married Dr Brice Smyth . . . Mr Andrew Gibson occupied the corresponding position on the Glasgow line of the John Burns Company.

Mr Gibson was an enthusiastic student of Robert Burns, and formed a Burns collection which was said to be the finest of the many notable Burns collections in the world. I remember how at all seasons he tried without success to interest me in his hobby – his 'Bobby hobby' he called it. At one time he was associated with a movement to erect another statue to the poet at some place connected with his early life, and Mr Gibson was indefatigable in his appeal for subscriptions. Of course in the large Scottish colony at Belfast he was very successful, and he admitted that the result was 'not so bad', which was going far for a man of his nationality . . .

XV

Custom House Steps Reached • M'Lean Fields Oratory
How We Got the Word Cloddin'

. . . Here I find myself at last at the Custom House steps, and I feel as if I could spend the rest of the space allotted to me in recalling the scenes which in my mind will ever be associated with that edifice. The idea seemed to be general from the earliest days of its existence that the Custom House was to do the duty of the Roman Forum . . . There was no really central open space in Belfast where an orator could practice his arts upon his fellow-townsmen previous to the building of the Custom House. There was, to be sure, a space known as M'Lean's Fields in the neighbourhood of St Malachy's, and it was acknowledged that when the oratory reached boiling point there was no more suitable quarter for a peroration,

followed by a baton charge . . . the technical term 'cloddin'' origi-
nated in M'Lean's Fields, the soil of which changed hands pretty
frequently in the course of an afternoon's discussion.[24] The 'clods'
were . . . by no means so convincing as the loose granite with which
the streets were macadamised in those days, so that the development
of a more convenient centre for asserting a citizen's claim to
freedom of speech made an immediate appeal to such orators as
had found the Fields tame. I think I am right in my belief that the
first riots Belfast had experienced since the 'Young Ireland' movement took place just after the Custom House had been built.

The Government of seventy years ago took a moderate view of
the future of the town and harbour of Belfast. The Custom House
and Post Office, with the Stamp Office and the Mercantile Marine
Board and Inland Revenue Offices were supposed to be amply
provided for in one building, and it was assumed that the Donegall
Quay would for long be found a convenient commercial centre for
every department. It was not with a view to give an imposing appearance to the building or to create an effective tribune for the display
of local eloquence that the building was raised high above the level
of the street; it was by reason of the chosen site being an imper-
fectly reclaimed marsh . . . The Custom House had to be built on
piles to give it any chance of stability. I do not suppose that the
inhabitants of the town were allowed any chance of expressing an
opinion on the site . . . or of suggesting that for anyone to be obliged
to climb from terrace to terrace to post a letter would be more or
less inconvenient; the Government . . . was a paternal one, and as
arbitrary in its decrees as were all the paternal authorities whether
belonging to the State, the Church or the ordinary household; and
the people had to accept like children what was offered to them,
without asking any questions or uttering a word of protest . . .

For many years the public business of the Post Office was
attended to by a solitary official. Postage stamps, money orders,

the registration of parcels, and the general 'counter' business of the department were controlled by an elderly man named Richardson . . . A more obliging person in a Government office I never met. If anyone wanted change for a sovereign or even a sixpence, he accepted it as his duty to provide the change in any form demanded . . . I remember good Mr Richardson very well, and also when two haughty young men took over his duties in a room at another side of the portico – quite a spacious room with a ten-foot counter and a trellised grille. But that was at a date before the postcard, the halfpenny stamp, the postal order, or the parcels post – before the Government had taken over the telegraphs, and when the telephone was thought to be one of the scientific toys that a young man named Edison was playing with at the other side of the Atlantic Ocean.

The Postmaster of Belfast was Mr O'Donnell Grimshaw, a most courteous gentleman, who at the same time carried on a considerable wine and spirit business in Donegall Street. It was thought absurd to fancy that the discharge of the duties of Postmaster would take up all the time of anyone; the office . . . might be accepted by any man with a spare hour or two. It had its equivalent in the office of Distributor of Stamps. A gentleman named Stannus – I believe he was a brother of the Dean of Down and the Lisburn agent to the Marquis of Hertford, the father of Sir Richard Wallace and the generally accepted original of Thackeray's Lord Steyne[25] – was the Distributor of Stamps. He had a very competent clerk in the person of Mr John Overend, who prevented him from being obtrusive to the detriment of the Stamp Office. For many years both in Britain and Ireland the post was regarded as a sinecure . . .

XVI

Custom House Steps Recollections • Rev. H.G. Guinness's
Oratory • Grousing of 'Jubilee' Wilson

While I stood at the head of the Custom House Steps when I was last in Belfast I tried to recollect the names of some of the orators to whom I had listened in my boyhood when they were holding forth at this place, but the only one that I should care to write about was the Rev. Henry Grattan Guinness.[26] He used to visit Belfast occasionally fifty years ago, but earlier I know that he spent a whole winter in a house which he rented near the Ormeau Road. His voice was not that of the raucous rhetorician, but of the educated preacher, and the impression he produced on me as a boy was of passionate sincerity; but his earnestness, though emotional, never degenerated into ranting. He had a really musical voice . . . there was not a forced or an artificial note in it. Now and again he spoke as one inspired; but he did not pour forth words like a torrent, as I have heard some great preachers do . . . Guinness spoke slowly, dwelling lovingly upon certain words, and he must have possessed to a remarkable degree the magnetic power that carries away a mixed audience. It was certainly amazing to witness the streams of people of all classes coming from all directions to hear him preach at 'The Steps' on a summer evening . . . It really might almost have been a Cup-tie final they were bound for. Mr Guinness as a writer was less effective than as a preacher . . . his subject did not make a universal appeal. The identification of nineteenth-century political incidents with the predictions of Daniel only arouses a languid interest in industrial circles nowadays . . .

The 'Steps' were regarded by other speakers as stepping-stones to political advancement, and one orator who was most assiduous in his Sunday afternoon appearances there, and who never failed to get some sort of an audience, entered the House of Commons.[27] Now and again . . . an attempt was made to turn the front portico into a Cave of Adullam,[28] and people who were dissatisfied with the Town Council held meetings of protest there . . . I remember the name of one Wilson in this connection . . . he insisted on commemorating Queen Victoria's Jubilee [1887] by building a row of houses which he wished to name 'Jubilee Street'. For some reason the Corporation would not give him permission to do so, and he declaimed his indignation on 'the Steps' . . . He became 'Jubilee' Wilson by popular acclaim, and was elected to the Council at the first opportunity . . .

I do not know if, with the increase of public parks in Belfast, the Custom House Steps have fallen into disuse as an oratorical mise-en-scène . . . But when the Custom House was built the only substitute for a park available in the neighbourhood was the Queen's Island. Some years later, however, it was announced that we were to have a People's Park, a fine space having been acquired for that purpose – a space on which every gift of Nature had been plentifully bestowed to qualify it for a park . . . with the exception of trees. This imposing acquisition on a nearer view seemed to bear a much closer resemblance to a prairie than to a park . . . The reclaimed land, a dismal swamp in winter, and a scrubby plain in summer, lying to the west of the Holywood railway embankment, was the Promised Land we were assured . . . It bore too striking a likeness to the desolate landscape in Holman Hunt's picture of *The Scapegoat*,[29] to be regarded by a rate-paying community as the nucleus of any demesne from which more could be expected than a suitable resort for snipe or plover. None the less it was referred to as the People's Park . . . in the summer, when it was moderately dry, the infantry of the garrison marched there for rifle practice, and in winter, when it was frozen over, crowds went there to skate. There were several hard winters in the 'sixties and the 'seventies, and at such times the place was crowded both by day and night.

My recollection of the winter of '67 enables me to state positively that the bracing properties of a mid-winter bath have been greatly overrated. I was deputed by some experimental schoolfellows to find out if the ice would bear. . . . I wonder, by the way, if the winters are as severe in Belfast as they were in a spasmodic way long ago. There was scarcely a Christmas without skating, though seldom a 'bearing' frost lasted for more than a fortnight, and I never remember being on the ice in the month of February . . .

XVII

Purchase of Ormeau: A Piano Story • Friars' Bush Cremation Effect on Botanic Gardens

. . . Up to the acquiring of the Ormeau estate the history of parks in Belfast was like the history of snakes in Ireland. There were none. And yet now this city is as well provided for in this respect as any park lover could wish. I cannot at this moment recollect who it was that was responsible for the purchase of Ormeau . . . it became practicable through the agency of Sir Samuel Black [the Town Clerk] . . . I have seen lithographs of the old mansion which stood at Ormeau, and I have a vague idea that I was brought to it when a child, and hearing of a sale of its furnishings.[30] Many years had passed, however, before I bought in a very humble dealer's shop an old-fashioned grand piano of English walnut inlaid with arabesques of brass . . . The name of Broadwood was on the plate with the trade number. I wrote to the firm . . . they replied that they had made it to the order of the Marquess of Donegall, Ormeau House, Belfast, in the year 1827 . . . since buying that piano I picked up several fine pieces of furniture which I felt sure came from the same mansion. For long I was puzzled to account for some admirable marble mantelpieces in moderately old houses in Belfast, until I managed to get an authentic account of the purchase of two of them at the breaking up of Ormeau. But beyond doubt the park was much better worth having than the house, and a monument should be erected at one of the entrances to . . . the man who secured the demesne for the use of the citizens.

But years before this happy transaction the Botanic Gardens, though not a public park, were available to subscribers, and most of the families living in the West End of the town were on the list – a family ticket was only a guinea. It seems extraordinary . . . that in all the years I lived in Belfast I never thought of enquiring as to the origin of the Botanic Gardens; but it is understood everywhere that visitors to a town know more about it than residents. When I first became acquainted with the Gardens there was only one lodge, for the Plains were really plains – uncultivated fields with a sheep track here and there. The Presbyterian College was approached by University Street . . . there was no exit at the lower end of the Crescent – Corry's Crescent it was called in those days. The fine conservatory was the chief feature of the Botanic Gardens, and it was looked after by a Mr Ferguson, who had the title of curator, and lived in a charming cottage within the grounds . . . I think that this Mr Ferguson had been connected with Kew when Hooker was the superintendent, for his eldest son, I remember, was called after the great botanist. About the mid-'sixties the subscribers to the gardens were greatly perturbed by an extraordinary practice which prevailed on the other side of their western boundary. The graveyard bearing the romantic name of Friars' Bush had ... become so congested that it was thought expedient ... to make a general cremation in various parts of the old cemetery, and as the holocaust was carried out in the most elementary way the neighbouring gardens every evening wore a pall of smoke of the most dreadful odour that could be imagined, so that it was impossible for anyone with a sense of smell to remain in the neighbourhood. I cannot say for how long this intolerable nuisance was continued; but the fact that it was permitted for a single hour throws a lurid light ... upon the free and easy municipal control which prevailed ...

With the development of the Plains a second entrance with a handsome lodge was made, and there was a succession of curators, none of them to be compared with either Ferguson père or his son Hooker who had succeeded him. Then there was taken on as an under-gardener, a young man, named [Charles] M'Kimm, who at once, by his quiet manner and thorough efficiency, became so great a favourite with everyone, that he was given the place vacated by Curator Johnstone, only he was not to be styled curator, but head-gardener. It was explained by the directorate that when a man was a curator he was above doing any real work, but a head-gardener was amenable to the control of a directorate. For twelve or thirteen years I was in the Botanic Gardens almost every day, winter as well as summer ... a more efficient man I had never met in any capacity ... He treated his flowers as if they were children ... he treated his children as if they were flowers ...

The tropical fern house built with his own hands in one part of the gardens I watched in all its stages. It did not cost the directors a penny ... it was one of the most perfect things of its kind I have ever seen. M'Kimm had educated himself in his profession so thoroughly that he was able to give the scientific nomenclature to the hundreds of plants that passed through his hands, even though the definition of the genus and species involved three or four Latin names. Among the many experiments that he made was one on the growing of the banana. I believe it was in 1885 that he showed me the bunch which crowned the large plant grown by him in his hothouse[31] . . . He also produced some beautiful new varieties of the 'pon-pon' chrysanthemum. And all this time . . . he was doing his best to make both ends meet for his directors. He was never given the chance of showing all that he could do until the Gardens were taken over by the Corporation. I saw him when I was in Belfast for a few days shortly afterwards, and he was elated at the prospect of carrying out his long-cherished schemes . . . Among the many attempts by the directors to make their accounts balance were weekly band performances and occasional firework displays. I recollect two fetes with balloon ascents. The first . . . was the enterprise of Dr Corry, of diorama fame, and the celebrated aeronaut, Coxwell, had charge of the balloon. Dr Corry . . . was not with the other passengers in the basket; he was reclining, as if in a hammock, in the netting just above. Mr J. F. Warden, the lessee of the theatre, was the entrepreneur of the fete of 1866 . . . the balloon refused to ascend, and the indignant crowd made such a fuss that the police had to be brought into the Gardens . . . A Revival meeting,[32] with free admission, served upon another occasion to crowd the Gardens, as also did a fete on March 10, 1863, when Albert Edward Prince of Wales, wedded Alexandra, Princess of Denmark.

XVIII

*The Petrified Waves on Quayside • Pet Ammunition for Riots
Stirring Days of '64 Recalled*

. . . I have a very vivid recollection of a Sunday riot in the region of
the [Custom House] within a few years of my becoming aware of
its existence . . . The roadway about the Custom House and on the
quay front was surfaced with smooth stones about the size of an
ostrich's egg. These were roughly rammed down, the only essential . . . being that the displayed portion should as nearly as possible
be assimilated to the crown of a bowler hat. These pebbles were
brought in considerable numbers from the coast of Scotland, and
they were cheap . . . the only expenditure incurred in the traffic was
for the transport, and as this was done by a class of boatmen who
would run across the Channel on a Saturday night and rifle a promising beach on the other side on the Sunday, returning, unless the
bottom dropped out of their boat, on the Monday, the Corporation
had not to impose a special rate for this scheme of paving. For years
in Belfast any large egg-shaped stone was called a 'paver', the
smaller size was termed a 'kidney'.

I do not suppose a more atrocious scheme of road construction
was ever devised by man . . . To cross the road was like fording a
stream by stepping stones, while the wear and tear upon the horses'
feet, and the wrenching of the wheels of all vehicles, were appal-
ling. Driving down to the berths of the cross-Channel steamers
gave a bracing foretaste of the bumpy and choppy seas usually met
with off the Isle of Man. The most seasoned passenger on a car had
to hold on grimly while passing over those petrified waves. But this
is only a criticism of the paver as a pavement. When considered
as a missile a great deal could be said in its favour by anyone

unprejudiced through having been unlucky enough to stop any such in full flight.

. . . I do not suppose there was a single stone of all the quayside that had not at one time been cursed by a carman or a cattle-drover, and what can be expected of a highway lying under such a ban? . . . When the orator at the top of the Steps became unduly familiar in his denunciations of all who disagreed with his doctrine, the disintegration of the roadway provided an abundance of argumentative material . . .

The habit had been formed previous to the great outbreak with the navvies engaged in excavating for the Dufferin Dock in 1864. I had seen dragoons clattering down Corporation Square and infantry with fixed bayonets forming cordons between the Northern Bank railings and the corner of Victoria Street, and I heard the names of the Custom House preachers who had stirred up the strife, before I was out of the nursery. In 1864 I saw a mustering of the local police force in Queen's Square . . . with chimney pot hats and walking sticks and rattles in their leather belts – and an hour later I saw the crowd of alien rabble sweeping everything before them . . . to loot every shop that was unprotected[33] . . . That muster of the old police force . . . had its pathetic side also, for it was their final public appearance as an 'exhibit' of inefficiency. I have no intention . . . to describe in detail the street fighting at various periods . . . but I have no hesitation in giving it as my opinion that the three p's – polemics, 'pavers', and police were responsible . . . Years after they were disbanded I came across some of them, and the stories they told me bore out all that I had ever heard of their incapacity and their venality and their dodges to evade their duties. The marvel was that with such guardians of the peace the town was ever at rest.[34] When it is remembered that it was just at this time that the town was starting upon those progressive strides which have been so well maintained, one becomes the more impressed with the fact that it is upon the character of the inhabitants rather than . . . the machinery of their government that the future of a town depends.

There was a commission of inquiry . . . the obsolete police force was disbanded and the Irish Constabulary – it had not its 'Royal' title until some years later – took charge . . . in 1865 . . . An immediate sense of security was experienced, though some years had still to pass before the shopkeepers in the principal streets largely abandoned shutters for their protection by night, and trusted to the vigilance of the double police patrol . . .

Having referred to the disturbance of 1864, I may remark . . . that it was the looting of his little shop in North Street that brought Mr William Gibson, the jeweller, to the corner of Castle Place and Donegall Place . . . known as 'Gibson's Corner'. The compensation which Mr Gibson obtained for his losses was of so substantial a character that he thought himself justified in taking over the business which had been carried on by a man named M'Cormick . . . He was a farseeing man and he understood the art of advertising in every shape and form. He had also a considerable amount of taste, which he lost no chance of displaying at International Exhibitions in Paris, Philadelphia, and Chicago. He started the Goldsmiths and Silversmiths Company in Regent Street, London, more than 40 years ago, having for his partner, Mr (now Sir John) Langman, a gentleman who possessed abilities far in advance of his own, the result being a large fortune for both. But while Sir John Langman was spending something like £50,000 with his ambulance in South Africa in 1901, William Gibson found a field for his energies on the Riviera. He had a villa in a much frequented locality, and when I was at Nice . . . I heard many reports of the spirit with which he had assimilated the traditions of that fascinating coast. I know that he had a number of hangers-on in London, but he was very generous with them all . . . When special constables were sworn in [1864] and provided with their batons, the leader of a patrol of some 50 or 60 was Alexander S. Mayne, whose death was referred to in the *Telegraph* a short time ago. His younger brothers, who were at school with me, pointed 'Sandy' out with justifiable pride . . .

XIX

Alabama's Hurried Flight Spoils a Projected 'Raid' Might have saved Millions

. . . I should certainly have written something about the hasty visit of the Confederate cruiser *Alabama*.[35] I cannot say in what year this incident took place, but I have a distinct recollection of its being so actively discussed at the R. A. Institution that several of the debaters were subjected to a penalty for their zeal . . . I suppose it was hearing the American War talked about . . . that gave us an interest in the *Alabama*. The word 'pirate' had been mentioned . . . that was quite enough to stir our imagination . . . We organised a surreptitious excursion down the Lough . . . There was a whip all round to purchase percussion caps at Braddell's, the gun-maker's, to suit the pistol which a member of our band possessed . . . I do not think that any of us suggested, whatever we may have felt, that it was the leaking out of this item . . . that caused the precipitated flight of the *Alabama*; but the news came on the morning of our projected excursion that it had cleared out of the lough when it was dark . . . The . . . caps we had bought were exploded by the shareholders, pro rata at the base of the statue of the Earl of Belfast, which in those days had not been deposed in favour of that of Dr Cooke . . .

XX

One-Time Picturesque Blackstaff · Graveyard as Playground
Old Linen Hall Parade

I have seen early lithographs in which were depicted high-class
Belfast citizens, with their wives and children strolling along
the favourite promenade available in the early part of the last century, which was on the banks of a picturesque river known as the
Blackstaff. I have also seen sketches showing fishermen making
their catches in the same stream; but . . . I was unable to identify the
topography of either of these pictures . . . So long as I can remember the Blackstaff was black and muddy and malodorous. It shared
the fate of many other natural features of the landscape in being
forced to yield its charms to the tyrant industry . . . [which] for
many years . . . was tyrannical beyond any experience of the present. In my young days the shops in High Street, Castle Place, and
Donegall Place were opened at seven o'clock in the morning and
closed at 8 at night – at 9.30 on Saturdays. The artist of the promenade scenes must have made his sketches on a Sunday, for only then
could our grandfathers and grandmothers have taken their walks
abroad. The only recognised holidays . . . were Sunday and
Christmas Day. Some shops put up their shutters at two o'clock on
Easter Monday, but the chief grocer was not among the number;
Forster Green invariably opened on Christmas Day as well! . . .

My earliest 'walking out' in Belfast took place . . . by the side of
a nurse who . . . seemed to think that a nice cheerful cemetery would
meet the requirements of any little boy for . . . outdoor exercise . . .
she knew of quite an attractive place . . . about the junction of the
Antrim Road and Crumlin Road. It was called the 'New Burying
Ground'. We found it a stimulating playground. There were surely

endless possibilities of hide-and-seek among the tombstones . . .
The only easily available alternative was the Linen Hall . . . the new
generation . . . can have little idea of the part that the enclosure
played in the life of the inhabitants long ago. The circular walk,
bordered by shrubs on one side and by trees on the other, was a
recognised promenade . . . The sylvan charm to be found within the
railings of the Linen Hall was highly appreciated when most business premises were inseparable from the household premises. But
I am sure that for more than twenty years before I left Belfast I never
saw a human being on that circular promenade which had once been
so lively – decorously lively, of course, with the crinolines and floun-
ces and 'Dolly Vardens'[36] of the 'sixties. At the height of its popularity, however, it was only slightly less gloomy than the cemetery.

When I stood on its site a couple of years ago, among the flower
beds and the sculpture of the gardens that surround one of the
most beautiful municipal buildings in the world, I was certainly not
conscious of any sentiment of fond regret . . . . I was only impressed
by the change which I perceived in the movement of the people . . .
The atmosphere which hung about the old Linen Hall was one of
repose – I dare not say 'sleepiness', for you would not have caught
any of the old mercantile class napping even after their Sunday
sirloin. But at the corner of Donegall Place, now fully occupied by
Messrs Robinson and Cleaver, there were a few dwelling houses of
the old type that imparted a note to the neighbourhood that I now
missed . . . The Mr Ferguson who lived in the house at the end, was
the finest type of a gentleman I ever knew – dignified, without an
approach to ostentation, courteous to everyone with whom he
came in contact . . . He rode a beautiful grey cob, as well mannered
as himself, and his seat in the saddle was of the old-fashioned type
of the equestrian statue . . . Mr Ferguson on horseback wore his
usual dress – a black frock coat and silk hat; he never wore gaiters.
The other house was occupied by a Mr Crawford . . . an accomplished

yachtsman and a lover of many forms of art. He was a member of one of the oldest Belfast families . . .

I suppose it was my recollection of these houses together with . . . the restricted promenade within the railings, and their high brazier bowls for the oil lamps they once carried, that induced me to associate that particular locality with an old-fashioned leisure, and to feel that the new crowd was one of 'thrusters'. While I was being elbowed out of the way of the people who were waiting to board a tramcar I recalled the time when some enthusiasts organised an open-air orchestra which occasionally performed just within the entrance gates of the enclosure . . . Very feelingly did they play 'I dreamt that I dwelt in Marble Halls' . . . I walked as slowly as was consistent with safety across the roadway and through the porch of the Town Hall, and there I found myself in the Marble Hall that the Bohemian Girl had dreamt of . . . [37]

XXI

How Solicitor Fooled the Court • J. P. and 'Carracty Curse'
Old Town Hall Recollections

The new City Hall has no legitimate claim to be considered [here] . . . But after visiting its magnificent public rooms I find myself saying . . . 'How very different from the old Town Hall that I remember!' . . . The Town Hall in Police Square was a ramshackle building with no more distinction about it than a second-class auction hall . . .

The Town Clerk ... was Mr Guthrie, an able man, who aimed at an annual reduction of the rates, and had his doubts as to the legitimacy of a municipal loan. The Council chamber was like a lodging-house 'lounge', of an inferior type. The Morgue and the Fire Station, as well as the Police Office and its cells, were close to the Town Hall, the Fire Station ... being a shed which nowadays might serve as a garage for a couple of cars if the chauffeur was humble-minded. In those days the head of the Fire Brigade was one Captain Shaw. He went direct from this Police Square shed to take charge of the London Fire Brigade and to re-organise it so that it became the finest in the world ... His name was immortalised by W. S. Gilbert in his libretto of *Iolanthe*. I used to see him occasionally when I lived in London. He had suffered the amputation of a leg, but it made very little difference to his activities.[38]

When the new Town Hall was built only a few hundred yards from the first, the general impression ... was that whatever progress might be in store for the town it would never ... necessitate more commodious municipal premises. That was barely fifty years ago ... It is never safe to make any prediction in regard to Belfast. One feature in connection with the building that was the new Town Hall in 1872, was the Petty Sessions Courts ... The court was held in a room about thirty feet square. The bench was approached from another room, and was five or six feet higher than the public space. The solicitors' desks, with their wooden seats, were two deep on each side, and no accommodation was available for the Press. As many as twenty adults could be crushed into a narrow strip behind a barrier, to represent the public. There was no separate Summons Court. When the trial of the prisoners in custody was over the 'summons' cases were heard, so that on a busy day the Court did not rise until six or perhaps seven in the evening. The clerk of the petty sessions was Mr Kennedy, a most able officer, his assistant being Mr MacHenry, equally capable. They had need to be on the alert when certain magistrates were on the bench. Not that there was ever any bias attributed to these, but a plentiful ignorance of law . . .

XXII

American Civil War and Linen Boom • Mushrooms of Commerce
The Constable's 'Patriotism'

Having mentioned one incident in connection with the American Civil War, I may be permitted to refer generally to the effects of that great conflict upon the staple trade of Belfast . . . In the mid-sixties many fortunes were being made in Belfast and many other parts of Ulster . . . It can easily be understood how a flax-weaving community should profit by the stoppage of the raw material for the cotton spinners. The blockade of the Confederate ports reduced the supplies upon which the cotton-spinning districts of England were dependent, so that the price of the inferior material they turned out became so nearly assimilated to that of the enduring fabric, that it was economical to buy linen instead of cotton . . .

As soon as the economic situation became apparent in Ulster . . . hundreds of acres were sown with flax, and there would have been hundreds more if seed could have been procured . . . Fortunes were made in seed alone, and the mills were working day and night turning out the finished material for the bleach greens. The merchants who supplied the bleach greens with their chemicals also made fortunes, as did the foundries who provided the machinery to the

mills . . . At the R[oyal Belfast] A[cademical] Institution four boys
out of every five were being apprenticed to the linen business . . .
the terms of apprenticeship were £100 for the first five years . . .
The impression I gained from all this was one of the stability of
war: the American War was . . . to go on for ever.

. . . 'Lappers'[39] became managers, managers became proprietors, and proprietors (some of them) became peers. Most of the
privately owned mills were turned into limited companies, and
clerks at £100 a year became managers at £1,000 – the foreign
correspondents in the head offices sometimes drew over £1,000,
I was told, and I stood breathless hearing it.

Of course this boom made no difference in the way of life of the
big firms with names . . . associated with the development of Ulster
for 200 years. The proprietors lived in the houses they had always
occupied. . . . But there were others who were carried away by the
dazzling prospects of a reign of linen. Palatial villas were built and
expensive furniture was bought by the van-load, and the cellar was
not neglected . . . The close of the American War did not mean
the closing down of many Belfast firms . . . There were some linen
houses – some that had not even a mill behind them – which
regarded themselves as so superior that the boys whom they were
condescending enough to accept as apprentices acquired the same
air of authority, and promptly cut the acquaintance of their less
favoured schoolfellows – this was a phase of which I had a mor-
tifying experience – but in the course of a very few years, the
gentlemen who had aspirations after the Viceregal Court found
themselves . . . applying for the protection of another Court, which
then was also situated in Dublin.[40] The mushrooms went the way of
all fungus, and the commercial atmosphere was the healthier for
their disappearance. . . .

All the American war did for Belfast was to give for some time
an extra impetus to the staple trade . . . The town was making

splendid progress when the war came, and while it lasted the rate of progress was accelerated; when it ceased there was no appreciable decrease in its advance, and since then it has rushed ahead far beyond what might reasonably have been expected . . .

What its future will be with the separation of the province from the rest of Ireland one need not hesitate to predict. It is better to be separated from the rest of Ireland than from Great Britain. That great Irishman, Oliver Goldsmith, wrote the allegory of the mad dog . . . The mad dog had its snap at Ulster, but,

> The man recovered from the bite,
> The dog it was that died.

Sir James Craig will, I am sure, prove the Pasteur of the Province.

XXIII

Greatest 'Fry' City Ever Had • The Theatre Fire of 1881 Toffee Vat that Overflowed

I have mentioned Captain Shaw and his connection with the Fire Brigade in Belfast. It was, I think, somewhere about 1862 that he got his London appointment, and the last big Belfast fire that he attended was that of the great warehouse of Dunbar, M'Master and Co. I am not sure if the firm was not at the time Dunbar, Dickson and Co. The alarm was given early in the night and before morning only a couple of the walls remained. Not many years can have passed before another large linen warehouse – that of Messrs Workman in Bedford Street – was burnt out. The brigade remained for two days pumping on the smoking ruins. In the same year there was a fine spectacular display in Victoria Street, not far from the Northern Bank, the flax store of Messrs Shaw and the large block of offices being destroyed in the course of a night. I believe that the hose was still playing upon the smouldering cellars at the end of a week. A considerable space of time elapsed before the bacon-curing premises of Messrs Sinclair in Tomb Street were burned. This happened on Easter Monday 1867, if I remember rightly, and I was old enough to criticise the display from a reasonable standpoint. I cam to the conclusion that what it lacked in flame was made good by smell. It was really quite appetising – that odour of frizzling bacon. Though it broke out at about eight o'clock in the evening, yet there was a breakfast time impression conveyed to us long past bed-time. The wind was from the south-west, and it rolled the clouds of greasy smoke up High Street and Castle Place, and even beyond the Linen Hall. I am sure that a connoisseur in perfumes would have been able to say from hour to hour when the hams were being overcooked and when the sides of bacon. I heard from some favoured persons who had been able to get to the entrance of Tomb Street, that the flames were at no time up to their expectations. They were spasmodic, and had not the real hearty flare-up of a bale of dry flax. Moreover the greasy smoke got into their eyes, so that it became tedious waiting for the roof to fall in. There was a salvage sale of the partially consumed stock shortly afterwards, and for some months there was no house without a plentiful supply of the products and by-products of the stores, the retail price varying from threepence to sixpence a pound. In those days, however, the finest ham, uncooked, was ninepence.

Of course a provision store, however combustible it may be, cannot be expected to make the same appeal to the senses as a wine and spirit store, though even the latter obviously cannot contain the elements of the thrill that must accompany the firing of a fully-stocked gunsmith's. I have a nursery recollection of hearing such a fire discussed, and I think the name of the house was Neill in High Street, but I am not prepared to say if there was any actual explosion . . . Very much later Messrs Robb, the drapers, gave us a magnificent Sunday evening entertainment, and the elements of the thrill were to be found in the proximity of Mr Braddell, the gunmaker. It was rumoured that in addition to several casks of the raw material, Mr Braddell had a good stock of fireworks, so that with the splendid possibilities in such a connection no one would be fool enough to go home before midnight . . . Even so far as it went this fire was a great success. There was the crash of floors and a long range of roofs falling . . .

At a fire in some saw mills in Eliza Street . . . there was some loss of life, one girl having jumped from a window that was somehow connected with the premises, but I do not recollect any other fatality . . . I remember very distinctly, however, the staggering effects of a fire at the spirit store of Mr Wilson in Victoria Street . . . a cask got separated from the lumber that were rolled into the middle of the street, and by some curious unexplained means the bung broke adrift . . . the people's feelings were not harrowed by any news of the contents of the cask flowing down a drain . . .

Another fire that might have been newsworthy if it had not taken place during school hours, was of a wholesale confectioner's in Donegall Street. The newspapers wrote quite callously about the overflowing of a vat containing the material for the manufacture of the most luscious toffee then on the market . . . The theatre fire of 1881 should occupy a place at the head of the list. This was the theatre which Mr J. E. Warden built in 1872 to replace the old playhouse . . . on the same site. Happily the outbreak did not occur, as most theatre fires do, during a performance. It was between

9 and 10 o'clock in the morning that the alarm was given . . . It was certainly the most imposing display ever given to the public in connection with the Arthur Square house, and it was fully appreciated by a large and discriminating public. When a theatre catches fire there is very little hope of salvage. The auditorium becomes a cauldron within an hour, and the large amount of woodwork in every part, and the many combustibles in the painting loft prevent even the most efficient Brigade from being able to save anything from destruction. Within a week Mr Warden had a stage fitted up in the Ulster Hall, so that he was able to fulfil the engagements he had made with the touring companies while the new theatre was being built. These included an Irving week, which was highly popular . . .

Among the more recent fires that I recollect was that which took place at Messrs Haslett's in North Street [which] spread almost to the point of destroying, in the auction rooms of Messrs Clarke & Son, a valuable collection of works of art about to be sold.[41] Happily, working under the guidance of two young art dealers . . . the porters deported the things, and only a few 'lots' suffered any damage. I was evil-minded enough to look for a subsequent salvage sale, but . . . bric-a-brac is not like bacon. I believe that everything fetched an uncommonly good price. An illuminated advertisement is always successful . . .

XXIV

When World First Saw Dunlop Tyres
Jeers Turned to Cheers as 'Billy' Romped Home

Walking over the Sussex Downs the other day I came upon a farm
cart drawn by an ox, and the sight of it brought back to my mind a
time when it was by no means unusual to see the like in the streets
of Belfast. If that were to happen in the same place to-day I
suppose it would be looked on as a way of advertising something –
most likely Bovril or Oxo . . . a prosecution might . . . follow by the
vigilant inspectors of the S.P.C.A. On fair days at least two of the
most primitive farm carts, an ox between the shafts of each . . .
[came] in from Whitewell . . . carrying farm produce – eggs, butter,
a chicken or two, and perhaps a belligerent turkey or gander. The
vehicle was of the exact type in use in Egypt three or four thousand
years ago, and only differing in a minor way from that in daily use
all over India with a draft buffalo in the shafts . . . The wheels were
a solid section of an oak log, divested of the bark and trimmed, and
the shafts passed under the square box that formed the body of the
cart, at such a slope to the rear that the rounded ends almost
touched the ground. The floor of the cart did not follow the slope
of the shafts, but was built up with a prop on either side . . .

I saw those primitive vehicles lumbering along the loose granite
of Victoria Street, and yet I lived to be present at the advent of a
vehicle that has done more to advance locomotion . . . than all the
auxiliaries of transport [since] Pharaoh and his host drove their
chariots heavily into the dry bed of the Red Sea. The athletic
meeting which took place on the Ulster Cricket grounds [1888],
when the little bicycle with the clumsy tires, ran out among the tall
spidery-wheeled machines with all the playfulness of a pony

among race horses, was an epoch-making event. Stevenson's 'Rocket' was no more important than the little bicycle ridden by 'Billy' Hume, which we received with derisive laughter . . . at first, but with a tumult of cheers later, when the ridiculous thing left all its spidery competitors far behind, and romped in I forget how many laps ahead . . .

Those who were present upon that occasion will remember how important a part the weather had played in making the triumph of Dunlop's invention an immediate one. There had been several days of rain and the track was so 'soppy' that the thin tyres of the five-foot front wheels of the competing machines sank up to the spokes in the ground, but the broad tyre of the experimental 'safety' skimmed along without leaving a trace. If the track had been hard, it is quite possible that its superiority . . . would not have been made so apparent . . . The victory was complete, though even the most active imagination could not have foreseen all that was to be brought about by the pneumatic tyre – the automobile and the aeroplane were both made possible . . . from that date. It gave man the freedom of the air just as the marine engine gave him the freedom of the seas. We have often heard of the irony of fate; but assuredly the grim gods must have smiled as that first roar of laughter went round the ground.[42]

Having seen that ancient ox-cart and that first pneumatic tyre I feel as Ulysses might have felt if, getting out of his boat at his island, he had seen the flag ship of the Italian squadron sounding for an anchorage. But there were intermediate types which I cannot but include among the curiosa of Old Belfast. One of these was the Royal Mail Coach which left the General Post Office at nine o'clock every night . . . It had the usual four horses, which were driven by a man like Sam Weller's father,[43] with a tall grey beaver hat and a coat of many capes. On the dickey seat was the crimson-coated and gold-laced guard, with his horn, and I doubt not, his blunderbuss, though the latter was not visible . . . The coach itself was like every other mail coach that one has seen in illustrations of the eighteenth century . . . Both the driver and the guard of our coach were quite elderly men . . . Never once did I see the horses stretching out for a gallop as such horses are shown in the old coaching pictures. They went up High Street at a slow trot.

For the appearance of this relic of a past age we were indebted to the curious scheduling of the trains to Dublin. There was no night train from Belfast, and the coach had to make an early morning connection at Portadown . . . I do not know in what year an arrangement was made with the railway company which put an end to the coaching of the mails, but I distinctly remember, when going to Lisburn one day with a governess, seeing the red-coated guard of the mail coach mounting to his seat on the top of the railway van in which the mail bags had been deposited. This van had the Royal Arms painted on the door. I cannot think that the position of this official was an enviable one. There was only a rail at the back of his seat, and he faced the engine, so that he must have had his breath taken away when the train reached a speed of thirty miles an hour . . .

The guard's perch represented, of course, an honest endeavour to make people believe they were still travelling by coach. In all the prints of the early days of the railway one sees the guard of the train . . . in an old coach seat on the top of the carriage. The build of the carriages for many years conformed to that of the horse-drawn vehicle, and even yet one finds in first-class compartments the leather arm-sling . . . supposed to mitigate the jolting that made coach travelling anything but a joy. For many years the best families would not enter a railway carriage to run the chance of sitting beside one of the general public. The best families travelled in the family carriage which was wheeled on to a roofless wagon. They thus enjoyed that seclusion which obviated the risk of molestation or contamination that the newfangled medium of transport suggested to their super-refined minds.

The passengers' luggage in those days and for long afterwards was piled upon the roof of the railway carriages. The trunks were carried by the porter up a ladder, and at the end of the journey they were sent sliding down a plank to the platform. There was a compartment for dogs – a low unlighted hole that would not allow any but the smallest animal to stand upright . . . At every station at which the train stopped one could hear the howls of the unfortunate animals. A journey to Dublin usually occupied five hours; but the 'Parliamentary' took seven over it. The 'Limited Mail' was put on some years later, and this enabled a traveller to be whirled to Dublin in three hours!

XXV

Irish Jaunting Car's Merits • Old 'Covered' Recalled The Era of the Private Coach

In my young days and for long afterward the car-stands were made up of 'outside' and 'inside' cars. The 'outside' car remains the traditional Irish vehicle. It has not been adopted by any other country, though I have come upon solitary specimens here and there . . . It is light and strong and easily controlled without the need for a brake. Its carrying capacity is amazing. Those that I remember in Belfast were constantly the bearers to the Giant's Ring[44] of six adults in addition to the drivers, and this with the 'well' space vacant . . . I have seen three on each side and two in the 'well' on many occasions and the horse did not seem overburdened. The manner of seating always appeared . . . to make an immediate appeal to a party of, say, four. The passengers on the one side were so completely independent of those on the other that they might as well have been in separate vehicles. I know that the etiquette of the jaunting car prevented one side from taking any notice of the other, and I never heard of a case in which the strict neutrality of the driver was violated. Of course when only two male passengers were on the car they sat on opposite sides and talked to each other across the 'well' . . . The outside car is still to the fore in Belfast but the 'covered car' has gone into the oblivion of the past.

The covered car . . . was more like a wagonette with a roof, only it had two wheels instead of four . . . It was entered from the rear, and its suspension was so low that it only needed one foot stirrup. On each side of the door there was a window, with a corresponding outlook in the front panels, the driver occupying a very narrow seat between the two outside. The driver was certainly constricted; but the passengers, if they did not mind their knees being very close as they sat opposite to each other, had plenty of room.

Really I do not remember any complaints being made against the covered car, but it became obsolete more than sixty years ago, its place being taken by the four-wheeler cab . . . There is nothing to be said against the four-wheeler, but it has always seemed . . . amazing that the hansom should be tolerated anywhere . . . It was inaccessible except at great inconvenience and the risk of carrying off some of the mud of the wheel, and though the seat was comfortable enough, yet when the glass was lowered in front in wet weather, one never knew what might happen. I never met with an accident through a hansom when living in London, but scarcely a day passed without meeting someone suffering from the effects of a breakdown, and gashed by the fractured glass.

The South of Ireland vehicle known as the 'jingle' was still to be seen now and again in Belfast in my school days . . . It used to be called the 'inside' car. It gave a passenger some sort of protection from the rain when the day was calm, but as the tarpaulin curtains swayed with every breeze . . . you should not accept the shelter of a jingle unless you are wearing a waterproof.

The omnibus services in Belfast were very elementary. There was a capacious two-horse vehicle plying between the Commercial Hotel at the foot of Donegall Square and the Botanic Gardens, and if one was not in a hurry it was a convenience to the residents in the western suburbs. Twenty or twenty-five minutes was occupied by the trip. Then there was a Strandtown service – Strandtown was Sydenham in my young days, with a Bunker's Hill in the vicinity – starting from the Bank Buildings. I think this was an hourly service. There was a County Down Railway 'bus, and I have vague recollections of an Antrim Road 'bus. With such meagre public means of getting about it is surprising that private vehicles were not more numerous in Belfast. A good many people kept their own outside and covered cars . . . In those days the greater number of tradespeople in High Street, Castle Place, and Donegall Place lived over their shops . . . the residential quarters were more central than they are to-day. Donegall Street was made up of private houses, as also was York Street, with its offshoots of Patrick Street, Great George's Street, and Henry Street on one side, and in the neighbourhood of the Northern Counties Railway terminus – it was known as Ballymena Railway – there were Meadow Street, Spencer Street, and Brougham Street. North Queen Street had many good houses, and the more central Queen Street and its neighbour, King Street, were wholly devoid of shops. The streets were aristocratic, with Fisherwick Place and Howard Street and Murray's Terrace in the immediate neighbourhood. Arthur Street was sacred . . . to the solicitors, and May Street to the doctors. Sussex Place and Chichester Street were wholly residential.

With this centralisation there was no need for many vehicles. In the fifties and 'sixties there was far more equestrianism than there is nowadays. I remember when every medical man of importance was a horseman . . . The people who . . . 'kept their carriages', lived as far away as Cliftonville or in some of the mansions on the Shore Road. I remember seeing more than once a real coach, with the coachman on the hammercloth, and the footman, standing on a small platform behind, holding on by straps . . . The ordinary but high-toned coach had its pair of horses, and two footmen in the capacious dickey behind. One family had powdered lackeys, but I only remember having once seen a Belfast coachman with the powdered wig of the magnificent person who drives the coach of the Lord Mayor of London. Several times, however, I have seen liveried postillions in action . . . When the Bishop was to take part in a marriage ceremony he was . . . driven to the church in a carriage with four horses with postillions . . . The Assize judges were invariably met by the Sheriff with a coach and postillions as well as a cavalry escort, and the judges' lodgings were provided with sentries and a military guard. Long before I left Belfast the four horses and postillions were done away with, but I suppose the military guard is still mounted at Assizes.

XXVI

*Pony-Drawn Cromac Water-Cart • Before the Days of Pipes
The Coming of the Tramways*

I have referred to the primeval ox-cart occasionally seen in the streets of Belfast fifty or sixty years ago; but there was another vehicle very much more common, which in design and utlity would seem to people nowadays to suggest an even more remote ancestry. This was the Cromac water-cart. It was usually drawn by a pony or an ass, but with an Indian draught buffalo it would have been the picture of the Madras water distributor. It was simply a twenty-gallon barrel lying on the framework of a small cart, and its equipment was no more than two strong wooden buckets with handles, suspended from pegs at the rear. I daresay that vehicle had at one time been regarded by householders as the most important of all on the streets, for it was the handiest means of distributing water to the houses that stood at any distance from the wells or the pumps before there was such a thing as a main laid down . . .

There were of course hundreds of people who shook their heads over such new-fangled ideas as a supply of drinkable water laid on in leaden pipes, and refused to let a drop pass their lips from so dangerous a source. When I was young every street harboured such conservative families, and the Cromac water-cart drew up at their doors, the attendant pulled forth the bung, and the crystal stream gushed forth into a bucket that had been collecting bacteria from the dusty streets for months previously, and was transferred into the big crock to be found in every pantry, sometimes covered, but more frequently (for hygienic reasons, we were assured) open and lidless. There was a notion that the water from the Cromac pump was particularly healthy . . . there was a sparkle about it which was lacking in the town supply. As usual, however, a meddlesome analyst came forward . . . and the Cromac brand fell away in popularity. I do not believe that the original supply . . . was in the least impure, but the risks of contamination in its delivery were so obvious that its use at the table should have been prohibited. The Cromac springs were used in the making of the best lemonade on the market at one time . . .

Before the introduction of the cast-iron mains there was a supply through wooden pipe. I remember seeing a very considerable

fragment of one of these unearthed about the entrance to Fountain
Lane more than fifty years ago. People who have a knowledge of the
topography of Old Belfast . . . will doubtless be able to say definitely where the spring was situated that provided the supply to the
fountain of Fountain Street, whence it was distributed through a
limited area by the wooden pipes. The fragment which I handled
was about two inches diameter in the bore, the thickness of the
wood being, I think, about six inches. Like many other wooden
pipes . . . dug up elsewhere, the oak of which they were made was
not greatly decayed, though it bore no sign of having been chemi-
cally treated to resist the action of the soil. Perhaps some person
may be sufficiently interested . . . to locate the various fountains
and pumps and wells by which the town of two hundred years ago
was supplied. I am sure that there was never any scarcity of water,
with the Cave Hill and Divis so handy; and if anyone had ventured
to suggest the coming of a time when Belfast should be forced to go
to the Mourne Mountains to meet the demands of the inhabitants,
that prophet would have been greatly discredited.[45] I do not know
when the scheme by which the water was brought in a viaduct from
the Lagan, to be distributed from an enclosure at the top of
Bedford Street, was working, or the area of the supply, but I
remember frequently coming upon the little conduit at the higher
ground above the river at Molly Ward's . . .

Of course the laying of the tramways in Belfast . . . brought
about the greatest changes in many ways to which the town was
subjected. I remember hearing the question of tramways discussed
from day to day in the train to Bangor . . . no inconsiderable pro-
portion of influential people were opposed to such an innovation.
A number of shopkeepers . . . were convinced that their businesses
would suffer materially owing to possible customers being whirled
past the shops . . . The Corporation . . . gave the powers to the
company that was formed, but wisely reserved . . . the right to take

over the system at the expiration of a certain period . . . The earliest service was . . . very sketchy . . . a single line of rails being thought adequate in many localities, and the permanent way . . . so indifferent that scarcely a journey was made . . . without the points being missed or a car derailed. The curve at the Linen Hall into Donegall Place was especially imperfect . . . The first manager was a Mr Totton . . . eventually he pulled the system into something like working order, and the routes were annually increased in many directions. At first the service was only between the Botanic Gardens and the Bank Buildings in one direction, and through Bridge Street and Donegall Street to the Antrim Road, with a branch down York Street, and another through High Street and Corporation Street to the Northern Counties Railway terminus. From the Botanic Gardens to Bridge Street occupied twenty minutes, and this meant a saving of five minutes as compared with walking. Later there was a service across the bridge, and the people began to get into the tramway habit. From what I saw on the occasion of my last visit to Belfast two years ago . . . they have now acquired it in the fullest possible way. I foresee the approach of that happy day when, with the cheapening of the price of electricity and the complete abandonment of pedestrianism . . . the profits of the tramcars will pay all the rates . . .

XXVII

*Recollections of St George's • Scholarly Dr MacIlwaine
His curate's work for SPCK*

I was interrupted in the itinerary I had promised myself of High
Street and Castle Place by . . . recollections of persons and scenes
which seemed to spring from the pavement at every step . . .

The Rev. William MacIlwaine, D.D., was the incumbent of St
George's . . . He was a scholarly man and a poet, as well as a student
of music. At the time of the Disestablishment of the Irish Church
he published an allegorical poem dealing with the situation . . . He
was said to have High Church leanings, but there was nothing of
the High Church ritual . . . in the services of St George's. Dr
MacIlwaine was the first in Belfast to preach in a surplice, the old
style being for the clergyman to go into the vestry during the
singing of the hymn prior to the sermon, and change from surplice
to black gown. Dr MacIlwaine was the first to introduce the chanting of the Psalms in Belfast. There was, however, in that church the
best music to be heard of any in the town, and the organ obbligato
to the chanting of the Psalms for the day, played by Mr Fred C.
Smythe, was invariably impressive . . . The choir was excellent at all
times, though as St Anne's had its anthem both morning and
evening, with, I believe paid vocalists, the Parish Church organist
had greater opportunities of an appeal to music-lovers . . .

Dr MacIlwaine's curate was the Rev. Edmund M'Clure. He was
a scholarly preacher, and left Belfast [when] . . . appointed Editorial
Secretary to the Society for Promoting Christian Knowledge, and
proved by far the most successful man that had ever been associated
with the office . . . What he did was to lift that class of its literature
which was meant to appeal to the young, out of the old rut in which

it was moving, and to place it before the public in a properly attractive form. For several years I was on his list of authors, though I had never met him in Belfast, and he told me so clearly exactly what he wanted that he had never to do any of the blue pencil editing which I thought might occasionally be necessary . . . . 'What we want is a story with a good moral tendency but no moralising, if you please'. Now and again he made a marginal note on my proofs . . . Under the guidance of Mr M'Clure the sales of the SPCK became enormous, and the profits beyond what the most sanguine could have believed possible . . . The books were well bound and illustrated by the best artists. Mr W. H. Overend did several of mine, and was afterwards commissioned by Mr Clement Shorter,[46] the editor, to illustrate a serial I wrote for the *Illustrated London News*.

No reference to St. George's would be complete without a word about the courteous sexton, whose secular office was that of Mace-Bearer to the Corporation. His name, I think, was James Morrow. He discharged his duties in both capacities with tact . . . Among the pew-holders in this church were several of the best known families . . . before the outlying churches of St Thomas and St James were built. Every Sunday the imposing porch was a background for carriages . . . Mr Ferguson, to whose house in Donegall Place I have already referred, had a pew, as had also his neighbours the Crawfords. The brothers, Doctors Charles and Henry Purdon, with their interesting households, came here from Wellington Place, and upon one occasion I remember being surprised by the appearance of Mr Frank Finlay, the proprietor of the 'Northern Whig', with his wife and her sister, in a prominent pew. Now Frank Finlay was an Unitarian . . . Dr MacIlwaine . . . forthwith preached a sermon . . . [on] the Unitarian creed [and] its errors . . . Everyone tried not to look in the direction of the Finlay family . . . They were more surprised than convinced by the well-meaning impromptu sermon . . .

XXVIII

Ulster Coat's Origin • Brought Fame to J. G. M'Gee
The Boycott Relief Expedition.

When I see the word Ulster spelt with a small initial . . . my memory brings me back to the place from which the earliest ulster emerged. This was the tailoring establishment of John G. M'Gee & Co., in High Street.[47] Travellers in every part of the world . . . have . . . 'blest him unaware' who invented the greatcoat which made a common noun of the name of the Province . . . some time in the seventies . . .

I remember very clearly seeing the window of that big shop filled with specimens of the magnificent garment produced by Mr M'Gee. Against the daintier garments in the other windows they seemed like a flotilla of ironclads beside a fleet of yachts . . . Many people still living . . . can recall the heavy overcoat which bore the name 'Dreadnought'. This was a modification of the splendid old Irish frieze of the forties or the fifties . . .

I saw Mr M'Gee wearing one of the earliest of his ulsters, and the sight was impressive. He was a very big man, tall and handsome – the father of handsome sons and daughters . . . To appreciate the true greatness of an ulster one should have seen the inventor inside one of his own garments. Mr M'Gee lived in Hollywood and for many years kept a yacht. He was a man of sound judgment on many matters, and good taste. He used to wear . . . a broad satin scarf with a fine pearl pin . . .

A few doors further up the street, at the corner of Bridge Street, was the establishment of Mr M'Gee's friend, Mr James Girdwood . . . Mr Girdwood had one of the largest furniture businesses in Ulster. Everything that came out of that shop was of the best quality, both as regards structure and upholstery. The carpets and

curtains of those days were atrocious as regards design, but for quality they could not be surpassed. At the opposite corner of Bridge
Street was the hardware establishment of Mr Robert Patterson . . .
a naturalist of considerable accomplishments . . . a Fellow of the
Royal Society . . . one of the originators of the Natural History and
Philosophical Society, as well as of the Naturalists' Field Club. He
wrote an elementary *Zoology for the Use of Schools*, which was
adopted by the Board of National Education in Ireland . . . Of
course, in pre-Darwinian days writers on natural history based
their works on assumptions which have long since been exploded.
But such books as Robert Patterson's inculcated a taste for study
and observation . . . The members of Mr Patterson's family through
the second and third generations inherited his ability and contributed largely to the researches of the societies associated with his
name. A volume on the *Birds of Belfast Lough*, which was most
admirably done, was written by Mr Praeger, a grandson of Robert
Patterson, I believe.[48] I have no doubt that the very mention of
these names will help the survivors of that generation of Belfast
worthies to recall many incidents of the past when they took an
active part in the development of the trade of the town – it had not
then attained the dignity of a city. They played a worthy part in
their day, and they should not be forgotten.

XXIX

The Royal Ulster Works • History of Marcus Ward's

I have already referred to some of the changes which have been brought about in Donegall Place since the days when we used to pass through it on our way to the rural glades of the Linen Hall, and, later, to that excellent type of workhouse architecture, the Royal Academical Institution . . . colloquially curtailed to 'The Inst' . . . Messrs Lindsay's Arcade . . . must have been built in '57 or '58. Mr Magill's print shop seemed to have been there always,[49] as well as Mr Mullan's, the bookseller's. This last-named was at times very attractive to me, but not nearly so much so as the shop of Mr Thompson, the confectioner. I consider myself fully qualified to write a whole chapter on the confectioners of Old Belfast, from Grant's, in Donegall Street, afterwards Heaney's, to Walker's in Bridge Street, across the street to Ogston's, then to Linden's, in Corn Market, and on to Marsh's, in Castle Place, only subsiding at Thompson's, in Donegall Place . . .

On the opposite side of the street nearest the Linen Hall was the Royal Hotel, and the next house was the piano warehouse of a Mr Coffey. But by far the most important of the business houses on the same side was that to which Messrs Marcus Ward & Co. moved from the corner of Corn Market. The town offices of Messrs Ewart were close to Marcus Ward's . . .

The house of Marcus Ward might well have a history of its own written[50] . . . It had the usual humble beginning, but the energy of the brothers who carried on the business in Donegall Place brought it into such prominence . . . that the works became one of the show places of the town. The retail business occupied a large frontage, and was of a high-class character. It included pictures as well as artistic books, leather goods and stationery, ledgers and the usual counting-house books. The premises extended back to Fountain Street, and on three floors were the printing presses, the drawing offices, the engraving rooms, and the many departments . . . For some years a picture exhibition of modern artists was held in the large gallery, and occasionally in those days of the big steel engravings a work likely to be popular with the masses was on view, and subscribers' names for the prints registered. The one work of sculpture which I remember in this gallery was an interesting marble *Elaine*, by Shakespeare Wood.[51] The members of the family whom I knew were . . . Francis, John, and William; there was another called Barrington, but he was not connected with the business. He became a school inspector in England, and his son, the distinguished K.C . . . told me that his father on retirement . . . had taken Orders and accepted a living in the West of England. Canon Ward died quite recently at an advanced age. It is interesting to note en passant that he was Treasurer of a Scholarship founded at the Royal Academical Institution to commemorate the famous Dr Blaine, and that he annually added a few shillings to the amount in hand to make the scholarship an even £10 . . .

For several years the business of the firm kept increasing with such rapidity that a move became inevitable, and the Royal Ulster works were built on the ground where I remember a private house named Bankmore to have stood, on the banks of the Blackstaff. It was afterwards a convent. Into the new premises the latest machinery was brought, and the enormous output of Christmas cards and the like soon exceeded that of any other house . . . The surpassing excellence of the designs and the superior technique of the colour printing were recognised all over the world. A London branch was opened, and another in New York. A staff of artists, sometimes numbering over thirty, worked under the superintendence of Mr John Vinycomb, a man of the greatest ability and good taste.[52] Mr Vinycomb's special branch was illuminated lettering . . . the great revival in this art, for which at one time Ireland had been celebrated, was due to him. From every direction orders flowed into the Ulster Works, until it seemed as if no 'illuminated address and presentation' counted for anything unless . . . done in the Ulster Works . . . Perhaps the most profitable 'line' of the whole business, next to the Christmas cards, was the South Kensington drawing-books and the school copybooks wearing the name of Vere Foster. Of these hundreds of thousands were printed . . . every year.

And it was at this moment, when business was at its best, that the house of Marcus Ward became divided against itself, with the inevitable result. I was in a position to hear both sides in the dispute . . . and sympathised with both. Anyone . . . acquainted with Mr John Ward must have felt that no abler man, or one more difficult to work with, could be imagined. He was nervous, impetuous, quick tempered, and even violent in maintaining his opinions. He was intolerant, not merely of slovenly work, but of work which contained the smallest divergence from the high ideal he had ever before him . . . More than once, when a design had been submitted to him – an illuminated page or a finely engraved copper-plate – he would say 'Excellent!' and then put a daub of paint on the one or a dash of the graver upon the other . . . 'but you will do it better the next time'.

It can easily be believed that such a man would be a constant source of trouble to his more easy-going partners, but I think . . . the first suggestion of a separation came from him. His half-brother Francis was as easy-going as John was difficult. The former was anxious to please everyone, the latter was determined to please himself first and let the others look after themselves. When the break-up took place the sum which John Ward took out of the business . . . was, I believe, £22,000.

The gentlemen who remained to carry on the undertakings of the house of Marcus Ward thought they were justified in looking forward to an easier time in the future . . . the designing-room breathed more easily, and Kate Greenaway[53] was ready to send in another score of the exquisite little pictures which she made for their Christmas cards, and every distinguished visitor to the town – it became a city through the exertions of Mr Francis D. Ward, the president of the Chamber of Commerce[54] – hurried to the Royal Ulster Works and expressed the heartiest appreciation of all that was to be seen . . . A younger Marcus Ward entered the office . . . an Oxford graduate and barrister of the Middle Temple, Mr J. Harris Stone, B.A., whose father was town clerk of Bristol, was brought to the firm for the development of the book publishing business, under the general management of a Mr Yeats. It was just when the reconstruction was complete and full of promise that Mr Vere Foster, whose name appeared on the drawing-books and copy-books, gave notice that he intended having them printed and published by another firm . . .

XXX

Beggared by Kindness • Career of Vere Foster
Associations with Belfast

Vere Foster . . . was a philanthropist if ever one lived in the nineteenth century.[55] Belonging to a great family and inheriting a considerable fortune, he spent his life and his money in forwarding schemes to benefit the people around him . . . I came upon a Parliamentary paper more than fifty years old, and learned from it that the scheme which Mr Vere Foster set on foot for paying for the passage and the outfit of Irish girls for domestic service in the United States had cost him £24,000 in cash, taking no account of his own time and travelling expenses . . . He gave the young women to understand that he was only advancing them the money. In order that they might not feel that they were going away as paupers he stipulated that they were to pay back out of their earnings the full amount that he advanced to them. The amount of the advances was £24,000. The amount of the returns was £8.

. . . He travelled all through Ireland, visiting the poorer schools, nearly all of which were Roman Catholic, and paying for the new roofs and new windows and new doors which so many of them needed . . . When anyone embarks on . . . philanthropy he is regarded by the great majority . . . as fair game for imposition. Mr Vere Foster gave me an example . . . illustrating very forcibly the opinion that prevailed as to the lengths one might go in 'stinging' him. A priest wrote to him explaining how dilapidated was the school-house in connection with his church. The roof had fallen in in places and one of the gables had been pronounced unsafe. The cost of the repairs was estimated at £400. Mr Foster went to the place and saw that the account which he had received was accurate, and he at once offered to bear half the expense of renovation, provided that the people of the neighbourhood paid the other half . . . After the lapse of a year another letter came from his Reverence . . . Trusting that the generosity of the donor would inspire his parishioners, he said, he had the whole work done, giving a personal guarantee . . . but now the people had broken their promises and he, their pastor, was at the point of being sent to jail for the debt . . . This piteous appeal was sent to Mr Foster's London address, but it happened that he was in Ireland when it reached him . . . he took a train to the place, sought out the schoolhouse and found it – in precisely the same state as it had been the previous

year. He found his Reverence and asked for an explanation . . .
'Well, sir', said he, smiling, 'I allow that it was a lie in the present, as
you might say; but it wasn't a lie in the future, for if I had got the
repairs done the devil a farthing would I have got of all that had
been promised me except your Honour's contribution'.

Vere Foster . . . used to travel third-class by rail, and he denied
himself an overcoat in winter. He lived in the most meagre way,
lodging in a single room – the 'bed-sitting-room' of the lodging
house – and he used to send out his cheques from here with no fire
in the grate!

Mr John Ward was a first-class business man as well as a first-
class judge of Art . . . he knew the value of having such a name as
Vere Foster on the covers of his books. It was he who suggested the
Vere Foster 'current-hand' headlines for the copybooks, and who
obtained the sanction of the Science and Art Department of South
Kensington for the drawing-books. It was John Ward who obtained
the sanction of Mr Poynter,[56] before he became president of the
Royal Academy, for the use of his name on the covers, and it was
John Ward's consummate knowledge of the technique of every form
of design that caused these books to be regarded in every part of the
world as unrivalled. The output of these books at the Royal Ulster
Works was enormous and the prestige which they conferred . . .
was immeasurable. The firm never recovered from the effects of
their withdrawal. An action was brought against Mr Vere Foster
and Messrs Blackie, the new printers, and being carried from court
to court for quite two years and lost by Marcus Ward & Co.,
with the usual piling up of law costs, the consequences became
more serious.[57] The firm had been turned into a company, with
Mr Francis D. Ward as managing director, and Mr Marcus Ward as
secretary . . . I do not think that the publishing was ever a great
success, though Mr Harris Stone tried to work it up in London,
where the chief warehouse was moved from Chandos Street to

Farringdon Road, and, later, retail premises were taken in the Strand. Mr Yeates gave place in Belfast to a new manager, and Mr Marcus Ward succumbed to his faith in faith-healing . . . In '96 or '97 . . . Mr James Moore was approached with a view of amalgamating his large business with that of the Wards. There was a Debenture issue for the first time . . . The situation could not be saved even by so intelligent a business man as James Moore, and the great house of Marcus Ward was wound up, the debentures being paid in full and the premises disposed of to Messrs J. S. Brown & Co.

With regard to Mr John Ward and his friend, Mr Vere Foster, it need only be said that in '92 the printers of the books were successful in their negotiations with Mr Ward for the sale of all his interest in these publications . . . Mr Vere Foster had, with his accustomed philanthropy, allowed his name to be a highly valuable asset in a business project, without any stipulation as to a possible pecuniary profit finding its way into his pocket. He assured me that from this final transaction he did not derive a penny. That transaction, however, made a breach in the friendship so long existing between John Ward and himself . . . The ability of John Ward was always as conspicuous as the philanthropy of Vere Foster. The former, released from the cares of business, hastened to Egypt, and made such an exploration of the Nile as had never been done before, and wrote a charming book on the subject, with illustrations executed from his own photographs. Besides writing *Pyramids and Progress* . . . Mr Ward issued a volume upon, I think, *The Nile to its Source*, and the photo process blocks made by W. and G. Baird must have been among the earliest book illustrations emanating from this firm. Mr Vere Foster continued to live in lodgings on a pound a week . . .

I should like . . . to pay a further tribute to the extraordinary knowledge of many arts at the command of John Ward. I never was so greatly impressed by it as I was during the opening of the exhibition of pictures at the Free Library. Mr Ward carried out all the arrangements for this exhibition . . . the finest ever held in Ulster.[58] He had an unerring instinct for all that was genuine in Art, and he had no hesitation in challenging anything . . . The exhibition would have been a very funny one if he had not been there . . .

XXXI

Belfast's Main Artery, or Rise of Royal Avenue
The Hercules Place That Was • Auctioneer and Upas Tree

I am afraid to say definitely that I remember the old Donegall Arms Hotel, in Castle Place, standing on the site now occupied by the Ulster Club . . . Being familiar with pictures of the place, with the mail coach waiting outside, I may only fancy that I saw the hostelry itself. But I have a clear recollection of the auction rooms of Mr Hugh Hyndman at that end of Castle Place, and of the shop of Messrs Simpson & Marshall at the corner. There were several auctioneers of the old school in Belfast in the sixties. Mr Hyndman was well known.[59] He was the father of Dr Hyndman, a solicitor, and a prominent Liberal . . . Dr Hyndman [once] remarked that Liberalism in Belfast was like the upas tree, throwing out its roots in many directions! Of course what was in his mind at the moment was the banyan . . . [60] Dr Hyndman was for some years the honorary secretary to the Philharmonic Society.

Having mentioned Mr Hyndman's auction rooms, I might refer to some gentlemen in the same profession . . . It must now be more

than a hundred years since the firm of Hugh C. Clarke & Son
began its career in Rosemary Street. I recollect the old gentleman
very well. He was genial and even merry during business hours,
and had thoroughly mastered the arts of the auction room. 'He
could wheedle a bid out of a black beetle', was the comment . . .
made by a dealer in my hearing. I had no personal experience of his
ability, but I heard a good deal about him while I was serving my
apprenticeship to the trade of collecting. Mr Clarke had several
sons, one of whom succeeded him in Rosemary Street, and the
others were in factories on the Gold Coast.[61] Mr J. C. Cramsie,
whose spacious rooms were in Waring Street, was an auctioneer of
the highest type. He was courteous, polite, and well informed on
many matters connected with his profession. He had some knowledge of art, which he took care to increase by his transactions with
those dealers who in those days were accustomed to travel with a
large stock of miscellaneous objects of art from town to town[62] . . .

Mr Hugh Hamilton . . . was a pleasant man who had graduated
in groceries. He became a member of the Town Council. Though
he had an occasional picture sale . . . he never acquired even a
passing acquaintance with art. I remember . . . [once] he was at
great pains to point out a mistake in the name which appeared in
the catalogue opposite a picture of a 'Rocky Landscape'. The work
was attributed to Rosa . . . 'I'm afraid that the printer has omitted
the surname to this picture in the catalogue', said he. 'I'm sure
you've all heard of Rosa Bonheur who painted the "Horse Fair".
This picture of hers is not quite in the usual style, but that makes it
all the more valuable.' Later in the day I enlightened him privately
. . . and as a return he sent me a catalogue of every sale in which
there was a picture.[63]

To continue my itinerary of Castle Place, which was deviated at
the old auction room of Mr Hyndman, I must say how reluctant I
should be to go round the corner into Hercules Place. In the old

days there were few people who thought it possible that such a thoroughfare as Royal Avenue . . . could ever have been evolved from the unsavoury Hercules Place. I have a very vivid recollection of this locality, though I do not believe I ever ventured beyond its entrance more than twice. It was the artery of the ancient town – the Irish quarter of Belfast, for Belfast . . . had its Ghetto in the form of an Irish quarter. Hercules Place, in spite of some thriving butchers' shops, was little more than a slum leading to slums. The old clothes traffic overflowed from here into Berry Street, North Street, and Church Street. On the other side there were slum lanes leading into Smithfield, that curious old market square of small shops, given over to rags and bones, second-hand books, and furnishings of a proverbially cheap and nasty type. It was scarcely safe to venture into that area in the fifties or sixties, even with an escort of the police of that period. But some years before the making of Royal Avenue Smithfield had been reformed. Several new buildings took the place of the old cabins, and such people as were under the impression that bargains were to be picked up in the Square were free to . . . attempt to get the better of a deal with the very sharp denizens of that happy hunting ground.

Personally I never lost hope of Smithfield, and upon no occasion did any of its inhabitants try to impose upon me. What I learned by my peregrinations in search of an elusive piece of old china, Ming dynasty for choice, or an unusual Sheraton chair, was that in that particular locality the most earnest habitués of the theatre were to be found. They had quite eclectic tastes in respect of the drama, showing no great particularity for the blood-curdling melodrama. But they were unanimous on the subject of the Irishman invented by Dion Boucicault. *The Shaughraun, Arrah-na-Pogue, The Colleen Bawn*, and the rest . . . they relished to the full. Really that 'Irish quarter' of Belfast was as distinct from the rest of the town as the Ghetto quarter of a Continental city is from the Cathedral square ... scores of the inhabitants ... had never wandered further from the centre than Arthur Square, unless there was a reasonable prospect of a riot ... The general constabulary orders when a riot was threatening were to shut in Hercules Place at one end and Church Street on the other. In August '64, when the funeral of some of the victims of the great outbreak was passing the entrance to Hercules Place [there was] a regular fusillade ... the squadron of cavalry that charged the mob were quite unable to clear the street.

The development of Royal Avenue made the greatest change that could be imagined ... The general impression up to that time was that the development would take place ... [on an east–west axis]; but with the startling popularity of the new artery it became plain that the Albert Memorial would no longer be regarded as the centre of the town, as it was in '69 when that clock tower was built. Royal Avenue gave an entirely new character to North Street, York Street, and the approaches to the northern part of the city.

XXXII

In the Heart of Belfast • Boy's Literary Quests Art in Donegall Place

... In old Belfast there were two or three eminent and enterprising publishers. The Blows produced a Bible, which now has a value in the estimation of collectors, and Messrs Sims & MacIntyre[64] printed many school books, the most popular of which was an *Elocutionist*, edited by James Sheridan Knowles, the author of *The*

Hunchback and other plays who lived and taught in Belfast.[65] There was also a *Thompson's Arithmetic*, the compiler being the father of the late Lord Kelvin, the most practical scientist of his day. He lived in College Square East, only a few doors from the house of the Rev. John Scott Porter, whose eldest son became, in 1881, Master of the Rolls in Ireland.

If Henry Greer, in High Street, was the most eminent bookseller in Belfast . . . the most popular was William Mullan . . . his name brings me back to my itinerary of Donegall Place. Mr Mullan had a large and varied stock at all times, and he was able to sell perfectly new books at a reduction of at least 25 per cent on the published price . . . Mr Mullan was the largest dealer in Ireland of 'remainders' . . . In the days when W. H. G. Kingston and W. H. Ballantyne[66] were among the greatest authors in the world . . . a good deal of my meagre allowance of pocket money found its way into Mr Mullan's till. And even when I had begun to suspect . . . there were greater writers than these, I could still spend a profitable half-hour and half-crown with old Mr Mullan; for some of the 'remainders' of the seventies became the rarities of the nineties. Mr Mullan had a son called Robert, who was in a publishing house in London.

On his return to Belfast . . . I think in 1879, he started publishing in partnership with his father. He had met, in London, Mr Jenkins, who had written a pamphlet entitled *Ginks' Baby*, and Mr Jenkins promised to put the new firm well on the way to prosperity by allowing them . . . to publish a novel of his . . . *Litchmee and Dilloo* . . . a story of East Indian coolies in the West Indian Island of Trinidad. Jenkins had been returned to Parliament for Dundee, and had married a Miss Johnstone, of Jennymount. He had been a member of a commission to inquire into the grievances of the Coolie in the West Indies; but his novel was a very poor performance, and its sale must have disappointed the producers[67] . . . An *Elocutionist* was, I think, the next performance of Messrs Mullan & Son, but the senior partner had made a very comfortable fortune, and seemed to have no desire to see it disappear . . . and the junior had ambitions beyond 'remainders' . . . Young Mr Mullan died, and his father followed him, leaving a larger sum of money than had been amassed by half a century of Belfast booksellers. Mr Mullan, the elder, was not merely a bookseller, he was a book-taster. He was always reading behind his spacious counters, and was able to give some sound advice to his clients.

Next door to the Mullans' was the fine art shop of Mr Magill, where that branch of the business known as 'gift books' was carried on with some success. But Mr Magill's chief business was photography[68] . . . An excellent portrait painter, Mr Douglas, was in his studio. Mr Magill had now and again a picture on view which was being engraved on the usual steel plate of the period, and subscribers' names . . . were registered in his office. I remember . . . seeing in this way Sir Noel Paton's *The Silver Cord Loosed*. Sir Noel Paton was easily a first favourite with the print-buying public.

It was only, however, when Mr William Rodman began business on the lines of Messrs Marcus Ward & Co., on the opposite side of Donegal Place to Mr Magill's, that the greatest works of Noel Paton, Holman Hunt, and Frederick Leighton were 'on view', and the walls of many mansions became enriched with reproductions of such masterpieces as *Mors Janua Vitae*, *The Light of the World*, *Hercules Wrestling with Death for the Body of Alcestis*, and many others[69] . . .

The enterprise, correct judgment, and good taste of Mr William Rodman gave his establishment a tone that was not to be found in any other in Belfast. Not only did he maintain the high traditions of the Wards . . . but in the course of a few years he inculcated, by the series of annual exhibitions in the gallery which he opened up in 1877, a feeling for good art that had previously been neglected.

Some of the most promising painters of the day sent their pictures to Mr Rodman's autumn exhibition, and while he gave a good display to these, he took care that local work should be given every chance on his walls, and the result was speedily made clear when the local artists started their Ramblers' Club, which developed into the Art Society, with an annual show of its own.[70] With the intelligent co-operation of his manager, Mr Cunningham, the Donegall Place Art Gallery has never been without some pictures of the highest class . . . I never saw an indifferent painting or drawing on its screens. When the new processes in black and white were being developed, Mr Rodman showed himself to be in touch with both experimental and developed work . . . clients . . . wise enough to take his advice in respect of some of the French etchers of forty years ago may account themselves fortunate to-day[71] . . .

In my very young days there was an excellent print shop in High Street, the proprietor being Mr Reilley. More than fifty years ago he moved to Dublin, and, with his sons, developed a large business in Grafton Street. I . . . have a very clear recollection of buying my first box of paints in his shop and receiving from him some kindly words of advice as to their application. I heard in Dublin that he had pronounced Belfast to be quite hopeless in artistic matters . . . Although there had been for many years a School of Design in College Square North, yet only a small amount of interest was generally taken in its work . . . The damasks of the previous century were infinitely superior to the newest, and the German taste prevailed over the native. The creation of the Schools of Art did much for the application of art to industry, and within recent years some genuine progress has been made. But knowing the condition of things in Belfast sixty years ago, Mr Reilley can hardly be blamed for trying to make a living in Dublin . . .

XXXIII

Doubles of Royalty • Belfast and Elsewhere
Actress and British Association • Imperial Hotel Episode

The Imperial Hotel had not the prestige of either the 'Donegall Arms' or the 'Royal' when Mr Jury[72] took possession of it . . . it was very early in the seventies when I overheard a commercial traveller tell a local tradesman that Mr Jury had that day paid off those of his relations who had gone into the venture with him, so that he became the sole proprietor. In those days he bore a striking resemblance to Albert Edward Prince of Wales[73] . . . Mr Jury did not trouble himself about this incidental likeness, though now and again he was chaffed about it . . . The Imperial quickly became a fine property under his management, Mrs Jury looking after the staff with a vigilance that brought about efficiency in every department.

Only one incident associated with the Imperial of 50 years ago seems . . . worth recalling. It happened in 1874, when the British Association met in Belfast and the President, John Tyndall, gave his celebrated address, which caused such a stir in the columbariums of the orthodox[74] . . . There was at the theatre a counter attraction in the very charming shape of a young actress named Ellen Wallis . . . She was a very beautiful girl and certainly the most capable emotional actress that had ever appeared in the part of Juliet, and the theatre was crowded to the doors night after night during her visit. She had rooms in the Imperial, as also had some of the distinguished savants who were attending the British Association . . . on the night of Miss Wallis's benefit, the jeunesse d'orée of Belfast were so carried away by her acting they escorted her, a thousand strong, from the stage door to the hotel . . . they made a demonstration in her honour in the front of the building . . .

Now, it happened the only room in the building that gave the actress a chance of responding was that in which the savants were partaking of the Spartan supper with which they recruited their energies for the morrow . . . She appeared at an open window and was greeted with cheers from the thousands in the street. In a few clearly spoken sentences she returned thanks for the great honour which had been done to her, and was making her bow when Mr Jury hurried into the room, and cried, 'Madam, I must ask you to retire to your own rooms; you have intruded into this one, and I cannot permit such an irregularity in my hotel.' He closed the window, leaving the actress . . . protesting that she had no option but to speak from that window, and offering an apology to the gentlemen at the table, who, if I know anything of scientific investigation, were delighted at the appearance in their midst of so exquisite an example of what centuries of Evolution had accomplished . . .

XXXIV

Unrecognised Festivals • Christmas–Easter Ban of Alert Forster Green • Belfast Bookseller Poets

Before proceeding with my memorial itinerary of Donegall Place, I should certainly not have omitted to glance at a shop at the end of High Street bearing a name . . . in every sense a household word in Belfast fifty or sixty – perhaps seventy – years ago. Forster Greene was a name which found its way into countless houses in many parts of Ulster . . . thousands . . . would scarcely be persuaded to drink any tea that did not cross his counter. I recollect his shop at the corner of Corn Market when it was a good deal less imposing than it became when the polished red granite columns introduced an element of decoration which seemed . . . inconsistent with the tenets of the creed professed by the proprietor. But as a company is said to be without a soul, and Forster Green became a company . . . the transaction relieved him from the responsibility of living down to the austerities of the Society of Friends . . . Forster Green was a quick-speaking and quick-acting man. The discipline to which they voluntarily subject themselves in their daily life may induce the Friends to apply a like code to those who are associated with them in business; and it was understood that Forster Green's establishment was conducted with a strictness that admitted of no relaxation . . . He refused to accept Christmas Day or Easter Monday as feasts in which his employes should have part, although he must have been well aware of the fact that those festivals put hundreds of pounds in his pocket; but, having made his conditions of employment quite clear, those who accepted such conditions had no reason, strictly speaking, to complain . . .

He did not adhere to the traditional dress of the Society, but . . . wore a glossy black frock coat, unbuttoned, and a special pattern of hat of the usual silk 'topper' shape, only low in the crown and broad in the brim – a compromise for the old-fashioned hat to be seen on the advertisements of Quaker Oats. He had a great appreciation of a horse. His vans were really, as we should say now-a-days, of too great horse-power. The animals were quite too spirited to be completely controlled by the rigid discipline of the establishment. When the driver got down from his place to deliver his goods, he took care to lock the wheels. In spite of this precaution, however, now and again the thoroughbred got his way, with inconvenient results. Forster Green was himself a good horseman. He had been ordered horse exercise late in life by his doctor, and he must have had some meteoric rides when his mount was approaching

Derryvolgie stables.[75] I am not in a position to say positively if he 'blended' his own teas, which made so great an appeal to his customers . . . The very mention of the name of Forster Green brings back to me fragrant memories of a lonely farmhouse between Millisle and Donaghadee, where I was entertained at a genuine County Down repast of soda bannocks, with butter fresh from the churn, and Forster Green's latest blend on the hob.

Forster Green's family were victims to that scourge of Ulster, tuberculosis. His son died just when he had left school. He had been sent to Algiers for a year, but the hope that the climate of North Africa would bring him healing was a forlorn one. Forster Green bequeathed a large sum to a hospital for consumptives.

Close to this celebrated grocery was the shop of Mr William M'Comb, the bookseller and poet. He was also registrar of marriages, an office which, no doubt, contributed to his success in both of the industries he professed. He had a large stock of high-class literature, mainly religious, and I am sure that he sold more copies of the Bible than all the other booksellers in the town. I fancy that the traffic in the old-fashioned 'family' Bible was never so great as in Mr M'Comb's day. He was a very religious man himself, and I have no doubt that he regarded as the highest privilege of his registrarship the opportunity it gave him of suggesting to the newly-made husband and wife that they could not make a better start in the way of a mutual purchase than . . . a Sacred Volume. Then, as a souvenir of the occasion he might suggest in a lower key Mr M'Comb's highly-decorated volume of poems – an ornament to the parlour centre table of the period, harmonising with the Berlin wool mats and in no way clashing with the vivid green of the rep curtains or the horsehair upholstery of the parlour. I acquired a volume of Mr M'Comb's poetry and read it with care. It was the verse of a thoughtful, pious and educated man – a man of many sympathies and much good sense. I am sure that the bride and bridegroom who bought the volume and read the contents never regretted this transaction, however varied their conclusions might be in respect of the one by which it was preceded.[76]

There was another bookseller poet in old Belfast, in the person of Mr James Reid, whose shop was at the corner of Victoria Street and Waring Street. I am not sure that this gentleman's outlook on life was as broad as Mr M'Comb's, and his metres were certainly more doubtful. He provided me with many 'slips' printed by himself, commenting on some of the notable 'events' of the day ... One that I remember dealt with a railway accident ... on a Sunday. His verses did not wholly convince me that no exception might be taken to his view of the catastrophe which attributed it solely to the displeasure with which Heaven regarded Sunday travel.

A much more literary bookseller was Mr Henry Greer, whose shop was just opposite Bridge Street. He was an old man when I was a schoolboy, so that he may have been in business in Belfast when the Battle of Waterloo was fought. I remember getting with some other books that had been disposed of at Mr Narcissus Batt's sale at Purdysburn, a copy of a volume of verse written by Thomas Romney Robinson and published in 1805, and Mr Greer told me that he remembered the author, who lived with his father in Belfast. His father was a pupil of Romney, and an extremely good painter. His greatest – certainly his largest – work is in the board-room of the Harbour Office.[77] It represents a muster of the old Volunteers in High Street, and includes portraits of many of the influential citizens of the period. Thomas Romney Robinson was only twelve years of age when his poems were published. He entered the Church, and achieved great distinction as an astronomer at Armagh Observatory. Mr Greer told me that Robinson had bought up all the copies of his poems that were available, as he was rather ashamed of them. He had, however, no reason for such a feeling. The verses possessed no originality, but they were quite as good as anything that appeared in *Hours of Idleness, by George Gordon, Lord Byron, a minor*, published in the same decade . . .

XXXV

Belfast and Darwinism • *Outcry from every Pulpit*
The Genius of John Perry • *When Army Refused Tractors*

I have referred to the meeting of the British Association in Belfast, in 1874, and I have a very clear recollection of the stir created by the address of Tyndall, the president . . . The general impression . . . was, I think, that the president had shown very bad taste in choosing Belfast as the centre from which he disseminated his doctrine according to Darwin but not according to Genesis. From every pulpit in the town came an indignant protest against the address, and when it was found that almost every other town adopted the same attitude of antagonism, the people who had been present at the delivery of the address felt that an unfortunate notoriety had been forced upon Belfast . . . The newspapers were crowded with protests and pamphlets swelled into tomes proving how untenable were the tenets of Tyndall and how disastrous the doctrines of Darwin . . .

. . . Within a dozen years of the controversy Belfast showed itself ready to welcome University Extension lecturers who went far beyond Tyndall . . . when Charles Darwin died, in 1881, his body was laid to rest in Westminster Abbey, not many yards away from the pulpit from which he had been denounced; and I daresay that the sermons in the English cathedrals, and the speeches of orthodox clergymen at Convocation in which the most cherished of the beliefs of fifty years ago are wholly rejected, are read without any uplifting of the hands in Belfast to-day.

I think it was a year or two after the great meeting of the British Association in Belfast that the Social Science Congress took place in Belfast. Lord Dufferin was the president, and in the course of his opening address he made some remarks on the subject of education . . . susceptible of an interpretation favourable to the Liberal party . . . Sir Thomas Bateson, who was the Conservative representative of the English constituency of Devizes . . . signalled his disagreement in a most dignified manner by rising in his place and leaving the meeting . . . Sir Thomas Bateson explained in a newspaper that the Social Science Congress was accepted as non-political, and as he felt very strongly that the president had introduced this element, he, Sir Thomas, had no option but to retire[78]. Sir Thomas Bateson was subsequently created Baron Deramore. His family had been for long in possession of Belvoir Park . . . He was a handsome man, a strong Conservative in politics, and an excellent speaker. Upon one occasion he gave Mr Gladstone a very bad quarter of an hour in the House of Commons.

Fifty years ago several of the most distinguished scientists were intimately connected with Belfast. Sir William Thomson, afterwards Lord Kelvin, was born . . . in a house in College Square East. He was . . . the most practical man of science of his day. His greatest achievement was, perhaps, the laying of the first Atlantic telephone cable, in 1866, though . . . a good many competent judges . . . would say that his greater achievement was the picking up of this cable when it broke. The deep-sea sounding machine, which is in daily use in ships in every part of the world, was his invention, as well as the standard ship's compass . . . in the wheel-room of every man-of-war and every great ocean liner. He was one of the greatest mathematicians that ever lived. One story that I heard from an intimate friend of his took my breath away. He was at breakfast in a country house where he was staying, and his host made a remark respecting the leaking of a certain water pipe, and asked Kelvin what he thought was the amount of the waste. Kelvin asked for the diameter of the pipe, and on the back of an old envelope made his calculations within the space of a few minutes. It turned out to be absolutely correct. More astounding still was his prophecy regarding radium. Many years before Monsieur and Madame Curie had discovered this product of pitchblende, Kelvin affirmed that such a substance must be in existence in order to account for an apparent discrepancy in the calculation he had made of the weight of the globe on the basis of all available data . . . Among his inventions in daily use in every household is the water-tap which bears his name[79] . . .

Lord Kelvin had for some years in his works, at Glasgow, a young engineer who came to him from Belfast, having graduated at the Queen's University, and worked in a local foundry . . . John Perry, one of the most brilliant workers in many sections of applied science. After spending many years with Lord Kelvin he was nominated to an important professorship in Japan, and later he returned to England, and was appointed a professor at the College of Science, South Kensington. He was elected a Fellow of the Royal Society, and for several years was on the committee . . . He renewed his acquaintance with me when I went to London . . . Several of Perry's electrical inventions were of great utility, and the appreciation of his teaching was marked by his election as president of the Electric Engineers.[80] At the annual dinner, at which I was present, he referred to the splendid possibilities . . . in many parts of Ireland for the production of electricity at an infinitely lower cost than was ever looked for in England. Lord Morris, in his speech later in the evening, remarked that on the president's showing Ireland should have a brilliant future. When I saw the late Mr J. C. White, at Tunbridge Wells, two years ago, he told me of the development of [a] scheme . . . for utilising the water power going to waste in Ireland for the production of electricity on a large scale, precisely as Professor Perry had advocated.

Professor Wyville Thomson was another great scientific man in Belfast more than fifty years ago. He occupied a chair at the Queen's College, when he was appointed to the staff of the *Challenger* expedition, and in the course of the cruise of that vessel in many seas carried out the deep water investigations with the most astounding results. So fruitful was the *Challenger* voyage in discoveries that after the lapse of nearly half a century they are still being discussed, bearing, as so many of them do, upon the latest theories in connection with biological science . . . [81] When Sir Arthur Conan Doyle was at Edinburgh University, Thompson was one of the professors. In his *Strand* biography, Doyle calls him 'Melville'.

Professor Sir Joseph Larmor, another Belfast student, made some of the most startling discoveries of the age in the fascinating field of electricity. If, as is generally accepted, the electron is the father of innumerable forms of life, assuredly Professor Larmor is the accredited father of the electron. He has been for many years a Fellow of the Royal Society, and I remember at one of the most notable of the annual dinners the enthusiasm with which his name and the mention of his services as secretary were received by that assembly of the most noted scientists in England.[82]

Fifty years ago the Queen's College was more than holding its own in the teaching of science. It was giving to the world some of the greatest investigators that have ever left any college in an industrial centre. Among its students who attained great distinction abroad I must mention Professor Joseph Longford, who matriculated nearly fifty years ago, and after taking his degree went to the East. His knowledge of China, Korea, and Japan and their respective languages and literatures and art is unequalled by any Englishman. His history of Korea is a standard work . . . On his return to England he was appointed to the Cambridge Professorship, which he still holds.

XXXVI

Famous Belfast Firms • Modest Beginnings
The Art of Hugh Thomson • His Debt to John Vinycomb

Two Belfast business houses with a worldwide reputation had their beginning well within my recollection . . . Messrs Robinson & Cleaver and David Allen & Sons. Not more than 50 years ago Messrs Robinson & Cleaver left the establishment where they had been employed, after serving their five years' apprenticeship in the old-fashioned way, and opened a small shop in Castle Place. I do not think that there was room behind the counter for an assistant . . . They were extremely modest in every way, but extremely competent and extremely industrious . . . There was no branch of their business that they did not understand, and, within a few years, it had so increased in all its branches that they felt that the estimates they had formed of the possibilities of development had not been over sanguine. I do not think they remained in High Street longer than seven or eight years . . . the name of the house had become so well known in many directions that they were doing one of the largest postal trades in the city; but . . . very few people . . . knew what its proportions were, and the creation of that imposing

building in Donegall Place startled a good many of us . . . There
was only thrift, industry, and intelligent advertisement to account
for the continuous success.

The same may be said of the second business . . . Fifty years ago
the firm was D. and J. Allen, and their printing business was in the
neighbourhood of Police Square. They turned out the few posters
and bills for the local theatre, and it was not, I think, until 1878,
when Mr David Allen's second son, Robert, entered the business
that the possibilities of specialising and developing this branch
[were] suggested . . . For some time so modestly did they move – a
single artist was more than sufficient to represent the staff engaged
in the development of the project, but once more a practical acquaintance with the technicalities of a difficult and exacting trade had its
reward, and in . . . a few years the works, with many additions, were
removed to Corporation Street, the largest lithographic stones
were stocked, the raw material for the colour printing was purchased
and ground on the premises . . . several artists who understood
something of the art demanded to produce an effective theatrical
poster were engaged, and in a marvellously short space of time the
name of David Allen & Sons was . . . found in the corner of thousands of theatrical advertisements . . . Mr William Allen was the next
to join the firm, and, lastly, Mr Samuel Allen. With the establishment of a warehouse off Leicester Square, London, there quickly
came the need for additional works, and, under the direction of
Mr Robert Allen, a large building was taken at Harrow, in which
the posters were produced and new ideas developed to meet the
constantly varying requirements of a greatly increased clientele . . .
Their industry and straightforward dealing had its reward. The
theatrical profession forty or fifty years ago was not just what it
is to-day, and to transact business with many of its members
demanded . . . the gifts of a successful diplomatist. But the Allens
faced the difficulties . . . and overcame them. Robert Allen married

in 1883 a daughter of the late Rev. Dr Workman, of Newtownbreda. He was an excellent musician and was organist of Dr Workman's church.[83] While still engaged in business he went to Trinity College, Dublin, got the degree of Mus. Bac., the examiner being Sir Robert Stewart. His brother, William, married Miss Cissy Grahame, an actress, once well known in light comedy.

I was not acquainted with any of the artists who worked for Messrs Allen in Belfast, but as I was made an honorary member of the London Sketch Club I met several who had done designs for him at Leicester Square. George Morrow, who has been on the staff of *Punch* for some years, was in the Belfast house for a considerable time . . . I was acquainted with his father many years ago and also his brother, both admirable men and possessing much of the artist's sense of humour.

But the man of whose name Belfast and Belfast's artists are worthily proud is . . . Hugh Thomson, who was in the 'drawing' office of the Royal Ulster Works within a few years of their opening. I have before me a letter which he wrote to me while I was still in Belfast after he had been taken to London to work for the Macmillans, and in this he paid high tribute to John Vinycomb, from whom, Thomson wrote, he had derived more knowledge of his art than he had acquired during whatever time he was at the School of Art . . . In 1878 . . . the artists at Marcus Ward's organised an annual picture show . . . at some of the earliest I remember seeing and commenting on some of Thomson's contributions. I do not know for certain the part that Mr John Ward played in establishing the artist on the staff of *The English Illustrated Magazine*, but I am sure that he had something to do with the transaction; at any rate Thomson got to London and began that series of eighteenth century illustrations which have never been equalled by any artist for delicacy of treatment and subtle humour . . . The eighteenth century atmosphere and the accuracy of the incidental details of every drawing that he made are [the] delight of everyone who has made a study of that fascinating period. I am pleased to know that that most competent of art critics, Mr H. M. Spielman, is collecting material for a volume dealing with Hugh Thomson's life and works . . . [84]

Mr Joseph Thomson's work in no way could be regarded as an attempt to adopt the style of his brother . . . He deserved to be considered on his own merits. He has a light touch, and a graceful humour. If he had been in touch with the publishers he would . . . have taken a high place among contemporary illustrators.

The two brothers Carey, whom I recollect very well at the Ulster Works, were also admirable artists . . . Like all the young men who sat by the side of Vinycomb, their draughtsmanship was faultless, and their technique careful, and wholly devoid of mannerism. They had imagination and humour. I remember very clearly watching John Carey engaged over an advertisement of Treloar's carpets . . . with as much sincerity as if he were engaged at a picture of the most heroic type.

The Dublin artists have always had so much to say for them-selves that it has . . . been assumed that 'art stopped short' at the Ulster boundary . . . far more artistic work of a high class has been produced in Belfast during the past half-century than in Dublin, or . . . all the rest of Ireland.

XXXVII

Greatest Irish Artist • Sir J. Lavery's Pictures
Belfast Portrait Painters • Distinguished Examples

. . . When the Nineteenth Century was in the flower of its youth, there was at least one local painter of unquestioned ability named Robinson. I have already referred to him . . . He was, as I have stated, a pupil of Romney; but he made no attempt to acquire that master's distinctive touch which allows of one identifying a Romney in any gallery of the Eighteenth Century. Robinson had characteristics of his own, and they appear in several of his portraits which I have had a chance of examining. But when he left Belfast there seems to have been so meagre a demand for . . . portraits that no artist of distinction thought it worth his while to settle in the town. When the full-length portrait habit was acquired by the successive mayors, the services of two painters were requested for the decoration of the Council Chamber . . . Sir Thomas Jones, the president of the Royal Hibernian Academy [and] . . . Mr Hooke,[85] who, I think, lived in Manchester.

I am not certain about his domicile, and it never was worth the consideration of his clients, for instead of bothering them to come to his studio to be painted . . . having obtained a cabinet photograph, he had it enlarged, and with this before him an accurate likeness was assured . . . Mr Hooke was a competent artist . . . all his portraits possess an equal amount of merit . . . he has never failed to catch the likeness that was the be-all and the end-all of the business.

Sir Thomas Jones stood on a higher level as an artist than Mr Hooke. His long connection with the Royal Hibernian Academy was greatly to the advantage of that institution. He had graduated in the studio of an English painter of eminence, and he had something of a style of his own. I fancy his best portrait is that of Mr Ringland, which must have been painted in 1869 or 1870, and which . . . hangs in the Directors' Room of the Ulster Bank in Waring Street. He had a firm touch and a good sense of colour . . . His portrait of Sir John Preston is the best of all in the Council Chamber[86] . . .

But when I faced all these old fashioned full length pictures and saw the effects of time upon the once brilliant colouring, I felt that I was justified in suggesting to the late Mr J. C. White, the preference for a commemorative portrait in marble rather than paint . . . which he had executed by Mr Sidney March . . . Mr White's portrait bust will appeal to his many friends who remain to regret his recent death.

. . . When I found myself facing a recent portrait by the most distinguished artist that Ireland has yet produced, I found myself breathing a very different atmosphere . . . Sir John Lavery easily takes a place among the greatest painters of the day . . . I have never seen more notable pictures than those which he painted in Algiers . . . Though a Belfast man Sir John Lavery has recently shown that his 'spiritual home' – to make use of Lord Haldane's phrase – is not within the irrevocable boundary of Ulster.[87]

When some years ago there was a question as to the locale of the collection of pictures of Sir John [*sic* – Hugh] Lane, who was lost through the action of Lord Haldane's spiritual homemates, in torpedoing the *Lusitania*, a circular letter was sent for the signature of Irishmen claiming the pictures for Dublin[88] . . . Sir John Lavery was a strong advocate of the claims of Dublin in this connection; but I really do not think that any stigma should attach to me for declining, in view of the recent wanton destruction of the Hibernian Academy and its contents,[89] to put my name to the petition . . . hundreds of the most valuable works of art in Ireland have been ruthlessly destroyed by those satyrs whose hoof-marks are apparent to-day in every part of the South and West, and to suggest that one's 'patriotism' should compel one to petition for fresh fuel to be added to the holocaust in the form of an incomparable collection of pictures, seemed to me to be going too far. If the appeal had taken the form of a requisition to house the pictures in Belfast . . . I should have put my name to it. Meanwhile, the collection may be insured in England at current rates, but no office would accept the commission at any premium were they within the boundaries of the Free State.

Among the excellent portrait painters whom I left in Belfast there were several whose claims to serious consideration were far beyond those of Mr Hooke. Mr Ernest Taylor had been in the Royal Academy Schools, and Mr Mackenzie was a gifted and conscientious artist whose portraits might have taken a place in any gallery. Mr Anthony P. Stannus was a constant exhibitor in the Royal Academy, and though his finest works were sea pieces, yet he painted many admirable portraits . . . An exquisite water colour drawing of his hangs before me as I write these words.[90]

Mr Arthur D. M'Cormick . . . came originally from Coleraine. He must have gone to London quite thirty years ago . . . he has not only painted some notable pictures, but as an illustrator of travel as well as fiction he has taken a high place. He was chosen by Sir Martin Conway, the Slade Professor of Art at Oxford, to do the drawings for more than one of his expeditions, and Mr J. Comyns Carr enrolled him in that very notable band, whose illustrations were so finely reproduced in the early numbers of the *English Illustrated Magazine.* No Academy illustration for many years has been without at least one of his pictures . . .

XXXVIII

Wielding the Long Bow • Miracles of Memory
Co. Down Woman and Queen Bess

I am pretty sure that, by the aid of almanacks and directories, it can be proved that my memory has been at fault in some of these jottings of the past. But I am equally sure that my mistakes have only been in respect of a year or two in dates and of a block or two in streets . . . All my life I have been notorious for a meticulous recollection of incidents, especially trivial incidents. I used to think that my memory was exceptionally good . . .

All of this is to lead up to my recollection of Dr MacCormac – not Sir William MacCormac, but his father . . . a familiar figure in Belfast fifty or sixty or even seventy years ago . . . He was like Tennyson's Sir Percival – 'Old and a mine of memories', but there was no sign of that mental decrepitude which causes so many octogenarians to confuse the incidents of their youth with those which they heard from their fathers or grandfathers . . . Dr MacCormac was a tall, well-proportioned man – in his prime he must have been as stalwart as his sons. He was short-sighted but did not wear spectacles . . . He seemed always to be thinking out . . . some problem that puzzled him. One subject that he had been investigating for years was . . . the frightful spreading of tuberculosis. He had had a vast experience of this malady, so common throughout Ulster, and he had formed his own conclusions respecting its cause and the possibilities of its cure . . . Fresh air and pure air were all that was needed to check the devastation of this plague, he affirmed in season and out of season, and like all the greatest investigators of disease . . . he was regarded as something of a crank, even by the majority of his own profession. They continued prescribing the climate of Madeira for consumptives, and close rooms and continuous warmth for those who could not afford . . . travel. For fifty years he preached the doctrine of a bracing atmosphere before it found general acceptance. He was the pioneer of the Alpine treatment and the open-air sleeping room. The stories told of his breaking the windows in the rooms of the poor people whom he visited in the back streets – windows that, like those in most of the cottages at the time, had not been designed to open – were numerous, all being designed to prove what a crank he was.

His elder son practised for a considerable time in Belfast, and on the outbreak of the Franco-Prussian War in 1870, went out with the first Red Cross Ambulance to France, and remained with the . . . French armies until the capitulation of Paris. He had with him . . . a son of Dr Pirrie, who had been a Queen's College student, and took his degree shortly after his return. From Gustavus Pirrie I got . . . some very interesting items concerning that memorable campaign. He subsequently went to South Africa where he died. I used to meet Sir William MacCormac occasionally in London. He was . . . present at the dinner of 'Belfast men' in the Trocadero, where I was their guest, and was deputed to respond with Sir William Abdy to the toast of Literature and Science. I had my chance of referring to Sir William MacCormac in a story of meeting someone in Belfast who talked of the great mistake Sir William had made in going to London, 'when he might have done so well in Belfast, where his father was so well-known' . . . I was sure that if Sir William returned to Belfast he would find sufficient friends of influence to make him practically certain of getting a dispensary . . .

XXXIX

Dead Man Who Groaned • Noted Medico's Weird Story
Belfast and Body-Snatching • Echoes of Burke and Hare

Recalling . . . Belfast doctors of long ago induces a recollection of
the dread which took hold of me in my childhood when I chanced
to meet any of the Queen's College students wearing their mortar
boards and gowns, as so many of them did on their way to lectures.
This is certainly the oldest of all the incidents that remain in my
memory . . . It had its origins in the gossip of a nurse with another
servant respecting . . . body-snatching . . . The woman would actually
hurry my sisters and myself into the sanctuary of the nearest shop
when one of the students – she assumed that they were all 'medi-
cals' and body-snatchers to a man – appeared in the distance . . .
There was a fierce quarrel going on between the medical men and
the Poor-law Guardians on account of the refusal of the latter to
allow persons who had died in their hospitals to be taken to the
dissecting rooms of their college . . . Our nurse had heard a word or
two about it . . . and she had really felt her responsibility increased
when in charge of such highly eligible subjects as I hope she
believed us to be . . .

When the practice of drawing upon the workhouses began I
cannot tell, and I suppose that a good many people are as ignorant
as I am to-day as to the sources of the supply for anatomical
purposes; but I know that there was a man who had a pony and cart
in the Queen's College district and whose business it was to collect
the 'subjects' . . .

Sir John Byers . . . was a friend of long standing. He was, I think,
one of the ablest men in his profession. His mother[91] had been for
many years the leading educationalist in Belfast, and the reputation

of her school in the Crescent extended to every part of Ireland. It . . . was a Belfast girl who first got by examination a doctor's degree. She was the daughter of a Mr William Gray, who was connected with the Irish Board of Works. He took a prominent part in the . . . Natural History and Philosophical Society as well as the Naturalists' Field Club. I think it was from the Methodist College that Miss Gray matriculated . . .

I have already mentioned the names of some of the early doctors who practised in Belfast fifty years ago or more. Possibly the most popular was Dr Haliday, a brisk, pleasant-mannered man . . . Dr Pirrie had a large practice, as also had Dr Dill, who for many years was coroner. Sir William Whitla had been house surgeon at the General Hospital in Frederick Street, and . . . gave a stained-glass window to the Boardroom . . . a very fine piece of work. Dr Whitla's *Materia Medica* was in the hands of students all over the world[92] . . . I was much more interested in his success as a collector of eighteenth century mezzotints and coloured engravings . . . no amateur ever succeeded as he did in picking up the choicest examples produced in England both as regards reproductions and original works. Some . . . possessed certain features that made them actually unique. One that I remember was from Thomas Stothard's[93] illustrations to *Paradise Lost*, showing the raven as drawn by the artist, but in a second, purporting to be from the same original, the engraver had seen fit to alter the position of the bird. Scores of these works found a place in lines on the walls of a spacious room in his house in College Square North, or in port-folios or on stands.

Another highly cultivated surgeon was Dr Murney . . . Courteous at all times and in all circumstances, Dr Murney was one of the most lovable of men. While he was still connected with the hospital he lived in the town, and was always available for the many demands made upon him; but for years . . . he went every evening by train to Holywood to live with his brother Henry, to whom he was greatly

attached; and as soon as he retired from active practice, he went to
live in Holywood with his sister. Miss Murney was a beautiful old
lady embodying all the dignity and grace which one attaches to a
picture by Sir Joshua [Reynolds] or one of Fragonard's Grandes
Dames. The Murneys belonged to a very old Catholic family, but
Dr Murney boldly faced the prohibition of his Church by becoming a Freemason, and I never heard that he forsook the Order.[94]

. . . Another great surgeon of the old days, Dr James Moore . . .
also was associated with the Frederick Street Hospital. He cultivated
with great success the brusque manners attributed to Abernethy,[95]
and he was always outspoken . . . whether in regard to art or hospital organisation . . . He was indefatigable in placing his undoubted
skill at the service of all classes in the community. He had an amiable
weakness for making friends among . . . celebrities . . . Dr Moore
was an excellent landscape painter . . . an honorary member of the
Royal Hibernian Academy . . . On his deathbed he was obliging
enough to read over and correct the proofs of the obituary notices
which he insisted on the gentlemen of the Press submitting to him.
His corrections were made, and the notices appeared ten weeks later.

XL

Presbyterian Champions • The Greatest of them All
Ulster Revival of 1859 • Coming of Moody and Sankey

There were three names in connection with the Presbyterian
Church to which great prominence was given when I was a boy, and
the greatest of these was Dr Henry Cooke, the second was Dr

Morgan, and the third Dr Edgar . . . Dr Cooke had been for many years deservedly all powerful in Ulster . . . He had faced the great Daniel O'Connell on the platform and routed him – for the time being. It is needless to say that O'Connell's final collapse was due, like that of every other idol of the Southern Irish, to the machinations of his own priests and party. It is impossible to read about O'Connell's Parliamentary and platform utterances without wondering how he was ever tolerated by respectable people . . .

Dr Cooke was a very old man when I heard him preach and I was a very young one . . . I was more impressed by his unaffected words and simple discourse on the subject of Faith than . . . any display of the eloquence one associates with the name of a great preacher.[96] He evoked love rather than admiration . . . his charity went hand in hand with his patriotism. I cannot recall the death of anyone in Belfast that caused so universal an expression of sorrow. It took place early in 1869. Some years later the largest procession ever seen in Belfast passed through the streets for the unveiling of the statue in his memory at the gates of the Royal Academical Institution. The site was well chosen. The statue of the young Earl of Belfast . . . always looked insignificant in front of so large a space as that laid down in turf beyond the railing . . .

The Rev. Dr Morgan was a small man, slow in his movements and in his speech. His sermon was unemotional – full of kindliness, and with an occasional homely phrase that suggested his addressing the members of his own family. He was greatly beloved by his congregation in Fisherwick Place, which included some of the most prominent men in the town[97] . . . The Rev. Dr Edgar was a strenuous advocate of temperance. He had a fine platform voice, not melodious, but certainly never strident. He was always forcible and convincing[98] . . .

There was another Presbyterian clergyman . . . whom I was brought to hear by a nurse. He was the Rev. Thomas Toye, of Great

George's Street . . . invariably alluded to as 'Tommy Toye' . . .
Everyone knows what sort of a clergyman . . . is accepted with such
familiarity by his flock. He was regarded as the 'daddy' of a happy
family – never standing on his dignity . . . always ready to speak
what was on his mind . . . Everything that such a man says is invariably acceptable to his hearers . . . it was the personality of 'Tommy
Toye' that counted, and of this fact he, being a shrewd man, was
thoroughly aware. Something out of the common was expected
from him week by week, and he rarely disappointed . . . He was
always on the best of terms with his flock, though not invariably
with his brethren in the ministry. I used to hear the quaintest stories
of his pointed allusions to the distinctive dress of the clergy, their
white ties standing in great need of laundering before he had done
with them . . . I am not sure that the report of his smoking a pipe at
the foot of his pulpit is correct . . . he certainly took snuff . . . He was
a little wizened man, and, wearing his black skull-cap, he appeared to
me a very comical figure. My experience leads me to believe . . . the
dialogue attributed to [such a] character is usually appropriate . . .
Tommy Toye was the man to influence for good the semi-maritime
inhabitants of Great George's Street and the region round about. I
have never heard it said that his preaching was above the heads of
his congregation.[99]

. . . Great George's Street Church was the centre of the neighbourhood most deeply affected by . . . the great Revival of more
than sixty years ago, though Dr Morgan was the most influential of
the clergy associated with the movement . . . The Southern provinces are supposed to have a very much more emotional popula-
tion than . . . any part of Ulster, and yet in the great Revival . . .
there must have been some of the most striking manifestations of
religious fervour known in history . . . Only within recent years has
anything like a scientific investigation of the natural laws associated
with panic and hysteria of a crowd taken place . . . In almost every

district where they took place, however, there were many cases of their influence for good.[100]

I have a very clear recollection of the earliest missions of the Americans, Messrs Moody and Sankey.[101] Their meetings in Belfast surpassed anything connected with a religious movement within the memory of anyone . . . thousands of people went . . . out of curiosity; but usually 'those who went to scoff remained to pray'. Mr Moody was not . . . a demonstrative or eloquent preacher . . . [He] was simple and sincere, I thought, without being in the least affected by it. Mr Sankey introduced the American organ and the cheap hymn book, and conducted the solo and choral department of the service. He had a pleasing baritone . . . a wickedly-inclined musical critic said that if he were in Grand Opera he would make a great hit . . . [as] Fra Diavolo.[102] I recollect entering a billiard room in Belfast when the Moody and Sankey Mission was at its height, and finding [it] . . . quite empty. So it had been all week, the marker told me . . . 'Never you fear, but they'll all come back', he said with a smile. And his optimism was justified . . .

XLI

Oysters and Singing • Belfast Delights of Sixties
Did Lady Macbeth Snore? • Denis Leonard at Hillsboro'

. . . Before the Ulster Hall was built the Music Hall and the Victoria Hall served on a smaller scale the purposes for which the larger place was designed. I believe that the Music Hall in May Street was built to meet the requirements of the Anacreontic Society, and within my memory its concerts took place there at intervals[103] . . . I remember being present in a room where old members conversed very freely about its past, but their conversation never got beyond an exchange of recollections of the delightful oyster suppers . . . they threw in their singing as part of their programme . . . by no means so essential to their well-being as were the oysters . . . Its concerts took place before I was in a position to attend such forms of entertainment; and the only entertainment I ever knew in the Music Hall took the very doubtful form of a bazaar . . . without the modern side-shows . . . someone might write a proper history of musical culture in Belfast, in which justice would be done to those amateurs whose enterprises materialised in the Music Hall.

I do not believe that I was in that same building more than half a dozen times . . . I attended a lecture on Oliver Cromwell by Professor Gibson of the Queen's College . . . I remember . . . the lecturer's old-fashioned elision of the w in pronouncing the name of his hero . . . The lecture . . . was given at the instance of the Marcus Wards . . . to advertise the picture which they had on view in Donegall Place, of the Lord Protector surrounded by his family listening to John Milton playing the organ in the background. The picture was being engraved, and the Wards were taking the names of subscribers for the prints.

Some years later I heard for the first time a very interesting series of readings given by a gentleman who was for a long time one of the best-known people in the old town. Denis Leonard came to Belfast as a solicitor, but previous to . . . entering that profession . . . . had a considerable experience as an actor, and had supported one of the Keans (Edmund, I fancy) as Richmond in *Richard III*.[104] He told me that Kean was so admirable a fencer that he would never let an incompetent actor take the part of either Macduff or of Richmond . . . on one occasion he was worried round the stage by

Kean, who whispered, when he had run him into a corner: 'Ha, I've got you now, you beggar!' . . . Mr Leonard had worked his way up to Macduff . . . he had at one time acted as the Second Witch . . . Denis Leonard had a very low-comedy face, and when, in the course of his readings, he came to a comic piece, he acted it to perfection. But his delivery at all times was so admirable that in the most tragic he never seemed out of place. He was a cultured man, of wide interests, and he occasionally wrote upon the drama above the signature 'Dramaticus' . . .

Upon one occasion Denis Leonard was given the very ungrateful task of reading what is termed 'the melodrame', in the oratorio of *Athaliah*[105] . . . as a sort of Greek chorus connecting the various numbers of the oratorio by an explanation. The effect is similar to . . . a foot note breaking up the continuity of an interesting passage in a book . . . the splendid music is rarely heard nowadays, though the grand March of the Priests is occasionally introduced as an orchestral piece.

Curiously enough, it was in the Music Hall that I made my first acquaintance with the ineffective character of [such] prose passages . . . This was in connection with the operetta *Preciosa* . . . produced by Mr Fred C. Smythe with some very competent amateurs in the vocal parts. The melodrama in the oratorio is, I think, founded upon Racine's great tragedy . . . but the *Preciosa* prose was the veriest prose.[106] It sounded like the explanation of the gentleman with the pointer who, in the old fashioned dioramas, came from behind the screen as the scenes jerked by on their rollers, to let the delighted audience know exactly where they stood, and what they were to expect if they remained quiet. In my very young days the figure of the diorama 'guide', as the gentleman was called, became familiar to me . . . his entertainment was the only one . . . thought safe for young people to attend . . . This blameless dissipation invariably took place in the Victoria Hall . . .

XLII

Belfast and Jenny Lind • Worshipping Golden Voice
Old-Time Victoria Hall Where Tom Thumb Held Reception

I am inclined to think that the Victoria Hall is somewhat larger than the Music Hall, though from the standpoint of architecture it would be bound to take a much humbler place ... before the building of the Ulster Hall it attracted most of the entertainments that took place in Belfast. From its open windows there floated the strains of Jenny Lind's incomparable singing,[107] and through the closed windows there floated ... a shower of stones upon the occasion of an election meeting. Here Tom Thumb held a reception, his master of the ceremonies being P. T. Barnum,[108] while outside there was awaiting the most charming little Cinderella chariot with its pair of grey ponies, about the size of a mastiff. In the Victoria Hall Dr Corry's Diorama of Ireland had a run of several weeks, if not months, and a young vocalist called Nellie Hayes sang in the costume of the colleen of the stage a number of lyrics plentifully besprinkled with 'mavourneens', 'acushlas', and 'asthores' ... At an earlier period Professor Anderson astonished packed audiences ... by his mechanical wizardry ...

He was followed by a couple of professional phrenologists – Fowler and Wells – whose 'reading' of the heads of various prominent citizens caused a good deal of discussion for a day or two ... Another Professor Stone gave an exhibition of ... mesmerism, and put his subjects through many exercises for the diversion of their friends in the front seats ... About the same period there were dioramas and panoramas illustrative of ... the Crimean War and the Indian Mutiny, as well as of the Holy Land, and the Rhine Valley ... Charles H. Duval, one of the best monologue actors I have ever seen, came for some weeks with a programme of amazing variety . . . I remember attending a Sunday school tea there with a magic lantern of wonderful 'dissolving views', and for a considerable time there was a Saturday afternoon prayer-meeting in the big room, and an occasional soirée of a colourable religious character . . . The Victoria Hall served the town well in the fifties and the sixties, and though I have not ascended that fine flight of stairs for very many years . . . I have several agreeable recollections of my adventures, illicit and otherwise, within its walls.

The earliest definite memory that I have of anything in the world was being carried in the arms of someone through a dense crowd that assembled in the big open space between the Northern Bank and the Eglinton Hotel when Jenny Lind was singing in the Victoria Hall . . . I required a very stern admonition to prevent me from joining my voice with those glorious notes that were listened to by that breathless crowd that stretched from Skipper Street to far up Victoria Street . . . A duet with Jenny Lind! The aspiration was surely a worthy one . . .

The entertainment in the Victoria Hall, with which I was forced to become most familiar, was the Saturday afternoon prayer meeting . . . a sort of by-product of the Great Revival . . . The meeting began about three o'clock and – I was about to write 'dragged on' – for a full hour. There was a platform at one side of the room, but neither pulpit nor parson . . . though frequently a clergyman of some denomination put in an ostentatious appearance . . . There was no programme and no ritual. Anyone who felt moved to a devotional exercise had apparently liberty to indulge it within certain limits . . . There was, on the baize-covered table of the platform, a glass water jug and tumbler and a small hand-bell . . . What I remember most clearly was my waiting breathlessly, with an eye on the clock, for the enforcement of that muzzling signal . . . An old man bearing the by no means unique name of Robinson . . . kept at least one eye upon the clock . . . He watched while the others prayed; the tinkle of the bell came with the precision of a time-ball, and the thing was done. Sometimes a hectic interest . . . was given to the proceedings by the persistence of a speaker; he pretended that he had not heard the tinkle, so absorbed as he was with the delivery of his message; but the referee . . . would stand no nonsense, and he gave the bell another and more vicious tinkle, and while I longed for some spirited evangelist to make a scene . . . yet the scene never came off. That was all I thought of at the age of ten on a fine Saturday afternoon, when I knew that cricket was going on in a field, and that a match was being played, while I was compelled to wait on one of the hard chairs in the Victoria Hall longing for the final sound of the bell. That was how precocious piety was evolved in the sixties. I was pushed as far as the precocity, but I fell short of the piety.

XLIII

*Duval the Versatile • Marvels of Quick-Change
The Ireland of Dr Corry • Contrast at Westminster*

If that self-styled 'Professor' Anderson, who came to the Victoria Hall . . . were alive to-day and to appear on any platform before the people who had been at Maskelyne and Cook's Egyptian Hall entertainment,[109] his feats would be received with derision. He had a very solemn and ponderous platform style . . . his wizardry was as feeble as that ascribed by Voltaire to the Witch of Endor.[110] But this opinion is of course founded upon an experience of the advanced forms of the art which he practised . . . If he invented the great rabbit and goldfish tricks, or the vanishing bird cage, he should be allowed all the credit that appertains to those mysteries; and if he was the first to fry eggs in a silk hat he should be regarded as a great pioneer of conjuror's cookery . . . His 'exposure' of the manifestations claimed by the early 'Spiritualists' took the form of a small drum swinging from a wire and giving forth taps now and again. In those days electricity as a motive power transmitted by wires was not in general use, but there were the wires and there was the drum, and anybody who considered that that apparatus made fools of the spiritualistic manifestations for which it was claimed that no human machinery was apparent, must have been easily satisfied. The scientific illusions of Pepper's Ghost[111] and the Vanishing Lady, to say nothing of Zazel, the chess player, were far beyond anything in the repertoire of Anderson . . . On his later visits he was accompanied by a very charming young lady violinist in short skirts. She played delightfully, and did the butterfly trick most gracefully as well as skilfully . . .

As for Dr Corry's Diorama of Ireland, which held the Victoria Hall in 1868, I believe it was really a patriotic venture . . . I do not think it proved remunerative. Dr Corry had a good deal of the philanthropist about him as well as of the patriot. I used to hear of his many acts of kindness to the humbler class of his patients in the neighbourhood of the Ormeau Road . . . The pictures of many of the famed beauty spots of Irish scenery were quite up to the average of dioramic art, and the singing and dancing of his well-trained 'peasantry' were as lively as anything on the Boucicault stage.[112] The Ireland of Dr Corry was the Ireland of Lever and Lover and Carleton – the Ireland with which the later exponents of Irish Nationalism would have nothing to do. Among all the Irishmen in the House of Commons when Mr Parnell was the leader of the

Home Rulers, there was not one who gave any evidence of the possession of what had always been regarded as Irish characteristics, with the exception of Colonel Saunderson, and he was the leader of the Unionists[113] . . . 'Little Nelly Hayes', as this young vocalist was styled in the bills of the diorama, had no prototype either at Killarney or any other show-place of the island: the begging colleens of Galway and Connemara did not invite English tourists to buy a box of specimens in short frocks of spotless muslin, supported by patent leather shoes with high heels. The real colleen had no match in slovenliness except in the slums of an Italian town . . . The whole thing was no more a box of specimens of anything that might be found in Ireland than the stage 'property' which the young lady colleen smilingly invoked an audience to buy. I never heard what became of Nelly Hayes and the rest of the troop. Let us hope that they all got married and lived happily ever after. Dr Corry was a tall handsome man, with the features and raven locks of the typical entrepreneur. He also wore the 'property' coat with the Astrakhan collar.

The last time I visited the Victoria Hall it was to see Charles H. Duval . . . by far the most versatile monologue entertainer of 50 years ago . . . He was the quickest and most convincing of all quick-change artists. He assumed a different dress for every impersonation, but he did so without leaving the platform; he stepped behind his screen, still talking in one character, and practically emerged from the other side, still talking, but in the speech and dress of quite a different person. He had a trustworthy singing voice – a light baritone – and he could go through the various tintinnabulations of Edgar Allen Poe's 'Bells' from stanza to stanza with an artistic force that I never knew equalled . . . He could give an extremely amusing parody of a melodrama, with several characters hurrying through the dialogue, and after appearing as the stage Irishman of the period, and singing something touching about 'the dear little, sweet little shamrock of Ireland', he would dance a *pas seul* in the form of an Irish jig, swinging his shillelagh in the most approved fashion, and twirling his caubeen also, à la mode, at the close.

He could appear as the 'Captain' of the day, and sing a song in glorification of his whiskers . . . and within a few minutes would be heard chatting in a falsetto behind his screen from the shelter of which he would walk in the evening dress, with the sloping shoulders and the flaxen chignon of the girl of the seventies . . . It seems to me on the verge of the uncanny that I should remember to-day the name he gave his coquettish young person. I am sure . . . a thought of her had never brightened my life for fifty years, and yet I can affirm with confidence that her name was Miss Bella Dashaway . . .

Upon the occasion of one of Mr Warden's annual benefits at the theatre, Duval appeared as a female character in a play with Mr and Mrs Warden. When on his way home from a very successful Indian tour he disappeared from his steamer one night in the Red Sea.

XLIV

Song that Saved 'Dorothy' • *Alfred Cellier's Career*
Organists of Ulster Hall • *The Methods of Dr Chipp*

I have a distinct recollection of the building of the Ulster Hall, though I had no idea what the building actually was . . . for several years. My first acquaintance with it as a going concern was when I was treated by a school friend to one of the Saturday Popular Concerts which must have been held in the mid-sixties . . .

As I am not now writing a history of the Ulster Hall, but only recording a few desultory recollections, I do not trouble myself with the exact dates of the Saturday Popular Concerts, or with the reason of the transfer of the evening of these festive gatherings to the Monday. What I recollect was the arrival at the R.A. Institution of a new boy . . . Herbert Chipp . . . his father was Dr Chipp, the newly appointed organist to the Ulster Hall. Herbert Chipp was a close friend of mine for a few years. He became a painter of distinction, and subsequently married a Belfast lady. He died when still young.

I think that Dr Chipp was the first organist. The great instrument had been presented to the hall by Mr John Mulholland, the millowner, who was created Lord Dunleath. Its cost I believe was £2,000. An embossed copper medallion above the keyboards is a record of the donor's liberality. Dr Chipp was certainly the most distinguished of the many organists of the hall. He was the composer of the oratorio of *Eli*, and of some of the finest organ music ever published. I believe he came to Belfast from Ely Cathedral[114] . . . I heard him perform upon many occasions, but I fear I was more impressed by the volume of sound than the performer's skill . . . I recollect very well the quick way in which he came before the audience to make his jerky bow, and boy-like, I did not fail to observe the slight turning-in of his toes as he walked. I knew nothing then of 'organists' foot', due to the heavy work at the pedals . . . it was still more observable in the gait of Alfred Cellier, who succeeded Dr Chipp in Belfast.

Alfred Cellier was quite a young man when he became organist at the Ulster Hall, and in the First Presbyterian Church, Rosemary Street. He was a brilliant performer, and I think that he was persuaded to adopt a less classical programme than Chipp was in the habit of choosing. 'The deep, majestic, solemn' phrases which the latter affected gave place to such comparative frivolities as 'The

Harmonious Blacksmith' or 'Cherry Ripe'. Cellier left Belfast in rather a hurry . . . but there was no whisper of any scandal . . . His subsequent rise to fame is a matter of musical history. He turned his attention to comic opera, and composed *The Sultan of Mocha*, which was something of a success in the provinces. One of the numbers, a lullaby, occasionally finds a place in a modern concert programme. Several pieces of his of a vaudeville type were done in Paris, where he lived for several years; but it was not until his *Dorothy* was produced in London that he became famous. I do not think that he profited by the success of the piece . . . on its first presentation it was pronounced a failure, and the full rights of performance were sold for a small sum.

Then an attempt was made to improve it by the addition of a song or two, and one of these, 'Queen of my Heart', sung by C. Hayden Coffin, seemed to take the town by storm. It at once changed a piece that was regarded by most people as an irretrievable failure into the greatest success in London, and for years *Dorothy* earned thousands of pounds for the lucky speculators. Cellier was encouraged to work at another opera of the same type, and in due course *Doris* was produced . . . I heard that it ceased to be remunerative after the first month of its run. There was no 'Queen of Hearts' song to tide it across the bar into the golden haven of popularity. Poor Cellier died shortly afterwards. It would be wrong to say that he died a disappointed man. I met him occasionally in London before the *Dorothy* days and he did not show many signs of being 'down in luck'. In those days if a man was in an artistic set he had need to keep a tight hold on himself, but like many other brilliant musicians, his friends were too numerous[115] . . .

Alfred Cellier had an equally talented brother, Francois. I remember his coming to Belfast for a week or two before his student days were over. He was fortunate enough to get into touch with Mr D'Oyley Carte[116] at the Savoy in the early days of the

Gilbert and Sullivan operas, and he quickly became the confidential adviser of the great impresario . . . He was for many years conductor of the Savoy operas. He died quite recently. I may mention in this connection that Mr Beckwith, who was for some time acting manager for Mr J. F. Warden, went to the box office at the Savoy and remained with Mr D'Oyley Carte until the theatre changed hands. He was a most courteous and efficient man, and a great favourite . . .

The Monday popular concerts had for a considerable time a large vogue . . . For months together unless one bought a ticket a full half-hour before the opening of the doors one could not get a seat, and no tickets were sold beyond the capacity of the building. The ordinary programme was made up of two or three organ solos, a couple of pianoforte performances, with perhaps a few violin or violoncello pieces. The vocal items were numerous; there was also a tenor, a baritone or basso, a soprano and contralto available, so that the two hours were fully occupied. But there were special occasions when the band of whatever regiment was stationed at the barracks performed, or where a noted musician gave us three or four solos. The first band was that of the 24th Regiment, which was then considered the finest of the line regiments . . . This was followed by one of the least noisy bands, that of the Buffs.[117] The conductor showed himself . . . well aware . . . that a brass band should not be heard within the confined space of four walls, and he chose his pieces accordingly; but the volume of sound that came from less considerate military bands made one feel now and again that the walls of the Ulster Hall would share the fate of those of Jericho[118] . . . When the Black Watch was stationed in Belfast . . . the ordinary band was supplemented by the pipers. They marched on the orchestra playing a strenuous strathspey, and kept moving, according to their custom. A plausible theory to account for this tradition is that the pipers knew perfectly well that when keeping in motion they had a better chance of dodging the missiles of an agonised audience. I never heard of a military piper being killed, or even seriously wounded, when on duty in Belfast, no matter how great might have been the provocation given by him to a musician with a good eye. But the range-finder had not been invented in those days. I doubt if, with such modern instruments of precision known to be available, the bravest piper of the gallant 94th would venture . . . to face a mixed audience nowadays.

XLV

Barton M'Guckin's Nose • A Transformation Scene
Soprano who was not Told • The Imitation Paganini

The vocalists at the early Monday Popular Concerts in the Ulster Hall were usually recruited in Dublin. The cathedrals of the metropolis were noted for their choirs and their training; and it seemed to be taken for granted by the Belfast directorate that local talent would be inadequate to fill the hall . . .

Amongst the instrumentalists by far the most popular was a Mr Levy, who was the leader of the Dublin Theatre Royal orchestra, and who called himself Paganini Redivivus . . . When he played in the Ulster Hall there was never a vacant seat.

I think it was in 1869 that Mr Robinson, of Armagh Cathedral, obtained a hearing at a Monday Popular concert for a protégé of his named Barton M'Guckin. He had been one of the choir boys, and had developed into a tenor of a delightful quality. I recollect the appearance of that youth who was destined to become famous, but

I cannot recollect the name of the first song which I heard him sing; but for that matter his memory as to the songs of his first appearance was as vague as mine. I was under the impression that one of them was Sullivan's [recte Balfe] 'Come into the Garden, Maud', but he thought I was wrong. It is a pity that one never quite knows what an actor or a singer is going to turn out or one would pay more attention to their debut. Barton M'Guckin had a marvellous memory . . . He was able to assimilate a long part after he had rehearsed it half a dozen times . . . His tenor was a most serviceable one, pure, and of a good range, without being at all remarkable. When he was at his best it had a robust quality that made his singing of the part of José in *Carmen* the best on the lyric stage. In the drinking song in *Cavalleria* its character was equally pronounced. I think that 'Salve Dimora', in Gounod's *Faust*, was transposed for him, but in the last duet in *Romeo and Juliet* he sang the high C in falsetto. When he made his first attempt in opera his acting seemed hopeless. It was more wooden than any Italian tenor then on the stage, and to say so much is to go pretty far. But he was shrewd enough to place himself in good hands . . . in a year or two he was quite a good actor. He had become so sure of the vocalism of every part he studied that he could give all his attention to its representation. I amused myself upon one occasion by keeping the score of an opera before me while he was singing, and I never caught him making a mistake of any sort, though he was so placed upon the stage that he had no chance of watching the beat of the conductor.

But there was one feature of his appearance in a romantic character that kept him out of an engagement for some time after he was fully qualified for several operas of the 'Grand' order . . . His nose was rather overdone by Nature in the way of being what Tennyson delicately described as 'tip-tilted like the petal of a flower' . . . He got concerts and oratorio engagements, but he had . . . set his heart upon opera. At last he succeeded, for good tenors are few, but his triumph was not yet. It came about through the agency of a candid friend, who took his courage in both hands, and told him what he should do, and he . . . got a new nose. But when he had done it, and made his entrance in a scene in which he was invariably received with applause, he did not get a hand. He had so transfigured himself that the audience failed to recognise him immediately . . .

He sang for many years in the Carl Rosa Company on tour, and three nights a week during their London season. They never had a more serviceable tenor, or one who made a more gallant appearance on the stage. He was certainly the best José who ever sang in English . . .

XLVI

Irving and Belfast
Lyceum Career Launched after Ulster Hall Visit
Story of Historic Episode

I am sure that anyone who was so closely in touch with the Ulster Hall of long ago as I was, could . . . go on for hours rambling about it . . . The further back the memories one records the better worth recording they are . . . Henry Irving came to Belfast and gave a reading in the Hall in 1878, and it was this that led directly to his taking over the Lyceum Theatre and starting on one of the most memorable theatrical enterprises of the Nineteenth Century . . . his coming to read on behalf of the Samaritan Hospital . . . brought about, within a week, his change from being a salaried actor in the Lyceum Theatre to be the lessee and sole controller of that theatre . . .

I was present when Henry Irving offered to come to Belfast and give this reading. The offer was enthusiastically accepted . . . But in 1878 he was, and had been for some years, a member of Mrs Bateman's Company, that lady having taken up the management of the Lyceum on the death of her husband, and although he was, as a matter of courtesy, consulted as to the plays to be produced, yet he understood that it was only as a matter of courtesy, not as a right . . . Irving had now and again felt . . . that he was unable to do himself justice on the stage so long as Miss Isabel Bateman was assigned the leading lady's parts . . . Although a charming actress, she was not nearly strong enough to represent the great Shakespearian heroines in the plays that would give Henry Irving an opportunity of appearing in the characters . . . represented by the great English actors of the past. But Irving had never forgotten all that he owed to the Bateman management . . . it was the cash contributed by another of the family that had kept the Lyceum open when the plays that were done at that house had proved unremunerative, even though he himself was in each and all of them; so when Mr Bateman died he had done his best for his executrix, remaining a member of the company of her choosing at a salary that was quite inadequate to allow of his paying his way – the way that he was obliged to take as the acknowledged head of the profession. But when Irving paid that visit to Belfast in 1878 he was in the Lyceum bill, and Mrs Bateman, in advertising the closure of the theatre for three nights, stated that she did so rather than engage any other actor to do Mr Irving's part.

Now, less than a year earlier Mrs Bateman had taken over the old Sadlers Wells Theatre in Islington without consulting Mr Irving . . . he felt very strongly that . . . he should have had a voice in regard to that new enterprise. That was how matters stood when Mrs Bateman inserted that advertisement which Irving interpreted as implying that if she wished she could have got an actor to do the part in his absence . . . When he returned to London he suggested the likelihood of the public taking this view of the situation, and the lady reminded him that she was the lessee of the Lyceum and that he was a member of her company . . . Within a week the newspapers made the announcement that Mrs Bateman had found that the direction of the two theatres was too much for her . . . and that Mr Henry Irving had agreed to take over the management of the Lyceum. That is the complete story of the breaking up of the connection . . . I had it . . . from Henry Irving himself as well as from Mrs Bateman. Of course each felt that the other had been wrong . . . 'You will never hear a good word of me from Mrs Bateman', Irving once said to me, and he was right. I was in daily communication with Mrs Bateman at Sadlers Wells for over two months in 1879, writing the pantomime . . . knowing as she did that Irving had had his first great chance of showing what an actor he was under the Bateman auspices – that he was risking nothing, but the Batemans everything, she felt . . . he had shown the basest ingratitude[119] . . .

For years there had been complaints on all sides in regard to the acoustics of the Ulster Hall, and some people who had Irving's ear had assured him that it was the most difficult building in the kingdom for a speaker . . . Irving visited the hall, and saw that all a speaker needed was to put himself more on a level with his audience . . . he got a couple of carpenters to work, and they ran up a temporary platform on a lower level . . . 'I can speak in a whisper now if I please', he said; and his confidence was not misplaced. Several times he whispered, and every whisper was audible at the furthest end of the building. He recited the full dialogue of the first 'Ghost Scene' in *Hamlet*, and let many of his audience see how it

should be done on the stage . . . if every member of the company
was as great an actor as Henry Irving. I have never forgotten the
expression on his face when he said, in response to Horatio's 'It
would have much amazed you', 'Very like – very like' . . . His greatest
effort was in 'The Dream of Eugene Aram'[120] . . . which most
critics had previously regarded as little more than a good vehicle
for the display of elocution of the blood-curdling melodrama
type . . . It was a study in psychology of the most subtle nature . . .

When Irving started management on his own account he took
with him as stage-manager a man who had lived in Belfast several
years, and who had married a Belfast lady. Harry Loveday had been
a teacher of music – the violin was his instrument – in Queen
Street. He afterwards went to a theatre in Liverpool as conductor
of the orchestra. He remained at the Lyceum so long as it was in
Irving's hands . . . He died less than ten years ago.

XLVII

Belfast Music Memories
Glorious Battle Song by Cork Man and American
Tietjens' Superb Soprano

Three musical performances out of the many that I recollect taking
place at the Ulster Hall remain in my memory as supreme. The
first was the duet from *Israel in Egypt*,[121] 'The Lord is a Man of
War', and the two bassos upon that occasion were undoubtedly the
greatest then living – Foli and Perkin. The former was always
alluded to by his intimates as 'Jack', and the idea seemed to prevail

that his name was John. It was, however, James, but being Italianised it became Giacomo, then shortened into Jack. Madame Foli never yielded to the Italian version in either form. She always called him Jim, but he did not always come when she called him, for whether as James, Giacomo, Jack, or Jim, Mr Foli, of Cork City, loved his freedom[122] . . . Giulio Perkin was an American basso profundo of the finest quality . . . He was not up to Foli's stature . . .

It would be impossible to describe the singing of Handel's superb duet by Foli and Perkin, with only a pianoforte accompaniment. One seemed to be listening, not to two singers, but to a host – a triumphant host. All the battle songs sound thin, even with a full orchestra, compared with this glorious number . . . I never was present when a greater demonstration was made in all parts of the hall. The audience stood up and cheered.

The second most notable performance . . . was the treatment by Madame Terese Tietjens of the recitative and aria from *Oberon*,[123] 'Ocean, thou mighty monster!' . . . Her delivery . . . gave one the impression of the Atlantic Ocean set to music . . .

The third . . . the playing of the Pastoral Symphony by de Jong's band in the same hall, an exquisitely picturesque treatment of one of the most exquisite compositions of the master . . . I have heard the Symphony played scores of times when *Messiah* was being given . . . I never listened to it patiently after hearing what could be done . . . by a perfectly trained orchestra under the guidance of a man of imagination . . . It suggested the starlight, the whispering of a breeze drawing near over a long stretch of pasturage, and then passing away into an unknown and mysterious distance – one did not know when it had ceased, leaving us alone under the cold stars. I did not know . . . the Pastoral was a tour de force of this band . . . some years afterwards, when I spent an evening with the conductor, I learned . . . he had always considered it their greatest achievement . . .

In Belfast by the Sea

The chief musical society of Belfast, whose concerts took place in the Ulster Hall, during its early years, was the Classical Harmonists. This society did some admirable work in the direction of oratorio . . . Their miscellaneous concerts were the means of bringing to the hall nearly all the great singers of the day. The first time I heard the Swedish soprano, Christine Nilsson, was . . . at one of the Classical Harmonists' concerts . . . At another, in February or March, 1869, the London Glee and Madrigal Union made up the greater part of the evening's entertainment. Their quartettes were their leading feature; but each of the members was a soloist of distinction . . . There were in the chorus of the Classical Harmonists two or three gentlemen who went to the Crystal Palace upon several occasions to sing at the Handel Festivals. There was never any lack of musical societies in Belfast, but until the Philharmonic was organised and took over the responsibilities of the Belfast Musical Society and the Classical Harmonists, there was no possibility of getting the best results, owing to . . . rivalry between the various associations . . .

XLVIII

Philharmonic Jubilee • The First Baton-Wielder
War-Cloud in Near East • Nearly Led to One at Home

I am surprised that no competent person has written a history of the Belfast Philharmonic Society. A good many less worthy societies have had their biographers. Even a bare record of its concerts during the fifty years of its existence would be extremely interesting to persons who have been from time to time among its members, to say nothing of the hundreds of thousands of people who, through its enterprise, have become acquainted with some of the master-pieces of music, choral as well as orchestral, and have been given many opportunities of hearing the greatest artists, vocal and instrumental . . . Such a volume would be not only of local but of general interest. If I had remained in Belfast I am sure that my ridiculous craze for writing books would have forced me to attempt something in this direction. The pleasure I derived from a regular attendance at the performances for close upon fifteen years was intense. During that space of time I never missed one concert, and I am convinced that there are many persons still living who could claim to have more than doubled my record . . .

. . . The society was due to the amalgamation of the Classical Harmonists and the Belfast Musical Society. But I am under the impression that there used to be a Philharmonic Society in the town some time in the 'sixties . . . The Musical Society had only been in existence for a year or two before it was absorbed, and I remember nothing about it.. there were always new societies being founded by music teachers . . .

I think that Henry Stiehl was the first conductor of the new Philharmonic – he was certainly the conductor in 1874, and I think the honorary secretary was a Mr Stirton, a very earnest and business-like Scotch gentleman . . . Stiehl was a Russian, but he had lived in Germany and had been a pupil of Rubinstein. He was not the thorough musician that a conductor should be; but . . . a great pianist, and a great enthusiast. He took more trouble over some Chamber concerts of his own than . . . the production of an oratorio by his society. No more perfect ensemble than he got together for the former could be imagined. The performances took place in the Minor Hall in the afternoon and attracted a very select audience. I do not think that he took any trouble to understand

Handel. The great master was not intricate enough to be thought worthy of the study of the early Wagnerites . . . The worst of his conducting was that it was not conducting in any sense . . . His baton described circles when he became excited, as he invariably did within the first half-hour . . .

When Russia was showing herself in a rather menacing attitude in regard to India . . . Stiehl put forward for rehearsal Glinka's *Life for the Czar* . . . [ignoring] those who knew how liable such a performance would be to a political interpretation in favour of the Czar[124] . . . If the committee had not taken very definite action . . . there might have been an unpleasant scene . . . As to his devotion to certain forms of music and his ability to interpret them on the pianoforte there could never be a doubt . . .

XLIX

Belfast Music Stories • The 'Little Goat' Class
Tale of Two Prophets • The Lapse of a Kettle Drum

When Henri Stiehl left (by request) the Philharmonic Society, he set up business on his own account . . . and gave a concert at which I am bound to say I heard some part singing, unaccompanied, of a quality beyond anything of the kind I had ever heard in the Ulster Hall . . . Stiehl was quite capable of working a chorus that included, as his did, twenty or thirty Germans, up to a very high level indeed. But unaccompanied part songs become monotonous, no matter how accurately they may be given, if they make up the whole programme . . . anyone with a feeling for good art must have felt sorry that so much that was excellent should be doomed to fail . . . Stiehl continued teaching in the town and seemed to be doing very well. Then he was offered a good appointment in Russia and hastened to take it up. I think he remained in Belfast altogether about five years.

The Philharmonic induced Sir Robert Stewart to accept the conductorship . . . He used to arrive in Belfast from Dublin late in the afternoon, conduct a practice, and return to Dublin the next morning . . . He had the College choir, and the two cathedrals to attend to, in addition to the work of his professorship and of his own choral society. He could not be expected to give more than a casual attention to Belfast. But it was Belfast that required most attention, especially as the orchestra was a young one. Several of the concerts in which the 'performing members' had very few chances given them of showing what improvement they had made, were admirable, and the performance of *Messiah* was particularly good . . . In the summer of 1878 that the announcement was made that the first concert of the autumn would be *Elijah*,[125] with Henschel singing . . . the prophet. For years Santley[126] had been associated with this work, and his interpretation . . . was regarded as one of the greatest of his generation, but it was known that Mr Henschel[127] was a baritone of great ability . . . Then suddenly there came the announcement that there was to be a three days' 'Musical Festival' in the hall in November, and that *Elijah* would be performed with Charles Santley in his own part! . . . But the Philharmonic *Elijah* came off and Mr Henschel showed himself to be a fine singer, subtle and emotional – very far from the Minor Prophet the Santleyites had predicted would be found.

A month later the 'Musical Festival' came off . . . It so happened that I had to go to Berlin for the second time that year – it was the year of the great Conference when Lord Beaconsfield and the Marquis of Salisbury sat at the table with Bismarck[128] – and on my return there was only rumour to depend on . . . Santley and the other professional soloists had been as great as everyone knew they would be, but I am pretty sure that the choruses were indifferent . . . Some . . . who had the best possible reasons for being interested in the financial side of the festival, referred to it in anything but a festive spirit.

Belfast has now and again had some professors of music who were without much staying power. There was a man named Cohen who was a very sound violinist, and as leader of the Philharmonic orchestra for several years was invaluable. He was able when any instrument failed to supply the missing bars with scarcely a pause . . . Such a thorough acquaintance with the score is not exceptional in a conductor, but it is not always to be found in . . . a first violin.

I recollect one occasion when Sir Robert Stewart's successor, Herr Beyschlag, was conducting an orchestral piece, there was a remarkable lapse on the part of the kettle drum, and this caused a sympathetic lapse on the part of one of the reeds. Beyschlag lost his beat, and when he heard Cohen playing the missing bars he became so confused that he caught the obliging bow, and, stepping down from his desk, began beating time for the kettle drum . . . The majority of conductors do their best to cover up the little slips of their instrumentalists during a public performance . . . Cohen was justified in rising from his chair and leaving the platform . . . Mr Cohen was organist of St. Thomas's Church, though how he got such a place in a Christian place of worship I was never able to find out. I heard a great deal of his shortcomings, both as a Christian and a choirmaster . . . He left Belfast very suddenly, and a year afterwards a firm of music publishers sent me a copy of some verses of mine entitled 'Homeward Bound', set to music (without the sanction of the author) by this Mr Cohen. When I explained to them the lack of this formality they sent me a cheque for the copyright. A year later still I heard that Cohen had been seen among the violins of a theatre orchestra in Liverpool. The last I heard of this erratic gentleman was of his selling newspapers outside a railway station in London.

Of a very different stamp was Mr Louis Werner, still alive and well, and organist of Holy Cross Church, Ardoyne, who was the leader of the second violins in the Philharmonic of old days. He was the most accomplished and certainly the most versatile of all the professors in Belfast. He was a fine organist, a capable pianist, and a composer of great merit . . . a master of every instrument found in an orchestra, and of some not usually found in an orchestra, as well. I remember when the Philharmonic produced *The Golden Legend*,[129] a 'tintinabulum' had to be found for the bell music, and Mr Werner had to manipulate the full peal of tubes in addition to his arduous work with the viola. More than once I have driven out to the Ardoyne church when the Mass music was sung by the artists of the Carl Rosa Company.[130] I shall not soon forget a certain Sunday in 1882 when I found in that church all the most earnest Protestants of my acquaintance listening most devoutly to such music as was not available to worshippers elsewhere . . . I heard recently that Mr Werner had received the Order of St. Gregory from Rome. This was indeed a proper recognition of his work. Unlike some Continental decorations, the Order of St. Gregory is one that is very sparingly bestowed, and only in recognition of exceptional merit.[131] It is pleasant to know that when the Carl Rosa Company are in Belfast they still go to the Sunday services at Ardoyne and contribute to the musical services there, where their old friend, Mr Werner, welcomes them as of yore.

L

Nightingales' Discord • Swedish Legation Scene
Nilsson in Ulster Hall • Memorable Belfast Messiahs

. . . Herr Beyschlag who . . . succeeded Sir Robert Stewart at the Philharmonic . . . was a most accomplished pianist, and the most painstaking accompanist. When I was passing his rooms in the small hours of the mornings during the week preceding a concert at which he was to play, I used to hear him practising the music of song after song. A less conscientious musician would have contented himself by running over the half dozen songs on the morning of the concert. I am afraid that he never got credit from the artists for all his pains . . . They did some 'interpreting' on their own account which Herr Beyschlag thought to be taking a great liberty with the text. Like so many Germans he had no more imagination than a Chinese tailor. It was always a pleasure to hear him play Beethoven, but I do not think that he would ever have become a good trainer of a large chorus. Anything more colourless than the well-known Fisherman's Chorus from Auber's *Masaniello*[132] became under his direction at one concert I never heard. I recollect also the slow tempo on which he insisted. The following year the opera was in the repertoire of the Carl Rosa Company, and Mr Goossens[133] gave it in the true spirit of the composition. Beyschlag returned to his native Frankfurt at the close of his engagement in Belfast.

. . . The most thoroughly efficient conductor of the Philharmonic was Mr Koehler. Certainly until he undertook the duty the full effects of 'Messiah' were never developed. The very first time that the oratorio was performed under his conductorship he showed his capacity. While all the other conductors had treated the various numbers in a disjointed way, ignoring the logical connection between them, Mr Koehler insisted on their coherence being maintained. I never heard anything finer than the choral singing under his treatment of 'Unto us a Child is Born'. The startling effects of the kettle-drums in the glorious outburst 'Wonderful-Counsellor' were produced just as Mozart, who, I think, did most of the scoring of the number, meant them to be; and certainly the full pictur-esqueness of the orchestration of 'He is like a refiner's fire', was never realised previously at any performance in the same building. For several years Madame Fanny Moody and Mr Charles Manners came to Belfast for the *Messiah*, and the soprano and bass solos were in keeping with the general excellence of the whole. I never heard the exquisitely simple 'I know that my Redeemer Liveth' sung with the same devotional spirit as Madame Fanny Moody imparted to it, and, assuredly, no more impressive declaration of the great recitative, 'Behold, I show you a mystery', than that which was due to Charles Manners' reading could hardly be imagined.

Like the great majority of musical societies the Philharmonic during the first twenty years of its existence was never quite free from debt, and the ingenuity of its financiers was greatly exercised as to the best means of getting rid of this burden which oppressed them. The most successful was a scheme of tableaux vivants, to illustrate a number of well-known songs ... The scene painter of the theatre and two or three of Marcus Ward's artists were engaged, and the result was very successful. Most of the leading amateurs sang the lyrics, behind the scenes, so to speak, and when the curtain was raised the living illustration was disclosed. In fact each stanza constituted what would now be called the cinema 'caption' or sub-title, only lacking the illiteracy which seems to be inseparably 'featured' in the modern entertainment ...

Other attempts to increase the interest in the concerts were made, one being the revival of some of the best known compo-sitions of the eighteenth century. The platform was furnished with

Chippendale and Heppelwhite, with sundry quaint mandolins and lutes to suggest the illusion as to the period. These were, however, only what might be called 'side-shows'; they were outside the true work of the Society wh[ich] was the production of classical work with an adequate ensemble . . .

While some of the great oratorios, including *Samson* and *Elijah* were performed, I remember more than one cantata by a modern composer featuring in the programme. *The Golden Legend* and Gounod's *Redemption* were among the more interesting of the works, which showed in a very emphatic way, the progress which had been made on the orchestral side of the Society's operations.

LI

Belfast Hotel Problem • *The Dickens Farewell
Dwarfed by Barry Sullivan* • *Byron's 'Waterloo' to Music*

More than once an attempt was made to organise an exhibition in Belfast, on the scale of those which had taken place in Manchester or . . . Glasgow. . . . About 1880 . . . the movement went so far as the formation of a guarantee list, and a very substantial sum was guaranteed should the project materialise. Plans were even made for the extension of the Ulster Hall . . . It was pointed out by some of those highly practical people who act as wet blankets . . . that to ask crowds to visit the town and then to find that there was no hotel accommodation for a tenth of the thousands who might reasonably be looked for, was to say the least of it, not businesslike . . .

But in 1870 there was a very nice little exhibition held in the Ulster Hall under the auspices of the Belfast Working Men's Institute, to find funds for the erection of the Working Men's Institute, which until recently occupied a handsome building at the corner of Castle Street and Queen Street. In 1876 there was another on a larger scale ... The machinery was driven by the neat double-cylinder engine, built by William Coates, Lagan Foundry, that was on view running in the window of Forster Green's, High Street. It was, of course, of a very local character, but it included machinery in action, and showed various industrial processes of great interest. There was also a picture gallery in the Minor Hall, which was contributed to by some Irish artists of ability, and among the sculpture was Mr Albert Bruce Joy's most charming 'First Flight', which was illustrated in the *Art Journal*. Mr Bruce Joy has executed several of the finest works to be found in the North of Ireland. The great Laird Statue in Liverpool came from his studio, and the portrait bust of Sir Edward Harland is one of the strongest works in marble in the Kingdom.

Before I turn my pleasant memories away from the Ulster Hall I must refer to some early readings which took place within the building ... Charles Dickens appeared in the course of his farewell tour reciting some of the most serious passages from his own works. I regret that I had not a chance of being present upon this occasion, but I was considered of too tender and susceptible an age to be allowed to learn direct from the author's lips how Bill Sikes killed Nancy ... I heard that this recitation took part on the night of Barry Sullivan's benefit at the theatre ... Barry Sullivan had scored a great triumph, the theatre being crowded in every part, while Dickens had only a meagre audience. I could quite believe this statement, for in later years I was made aware of the position which Barry Sullivan occupied ... in the estimation of theatre-goers in Belfast ...

One well-known reader I recollect hearing in the Ulster Hall. He was Mr J. M. W. Bellew[134] . . . the original of Dickens's 'Mr Honeyman' [recte Thackeray], the handsome preacher who was said to gain more hearts than souls . . . Bellew did not impress me as a boy, and now that I can analyse his art I am convinced that I did well to be impassive. His methods would be received with derision nowadays. For instance, in reading Pope's adaptation of Hadrian's 'Anima, blandula, vagula', which he called 'the Dying Christian to his Soul', the reader provided a white-robed choir of ladies, who sat behind his desk, and when he came to the line, 'Hark! They whisper, angels say – sister-spirit, come away'! rose and sang the words attributed to the angels quite prettily. Now everybody knows that the dying Christian alone could hear the angels whisper. That line can be made inexpressibly beautiful if read in the spirit of the poem . . .

Then, again, before he read Byron's stanzas from *Childe Harold* on the Field of Waterloo, he arranged for the organist to play up a waltz . . . the 'sound of revelry by night', and when he came to 'Hush! Hark! A deep sound strikes like a rising knell', he need not have added the question of the poem, 'Did ye not hear it?' for the organist took very good care that low G, with an open swell, was heard far and wide . . . He took very good care to have the bugle sounding the charge 'Half a league, half a league, half a league onward!' Mr Pennington, who only died last year, used to act with Miss Wallis, and between the acts in one of the plays, appear in the hussar tunic the same as he had worn in the charge of the Light Brigade, brought on his bugler, and when he came to 'flashed all their sabres bare!' he flashed his own good sabre as bare as the best of them. That was also an artistic mistake, 'not but what I owns, relishing', as Mrs Middlewick says of leeks, in *Our Boys* . . .

I read some months ago a very interesting account, in the *Belfast Telegraph*, of the recital given by Mr Alex. S. Mayne, in the Ulster Hall, and subsequently in St. James's Hall, London. I was present upon the former occasion . . . He had met with some serious reverses in business . . . I saw no reason why he should not have done very well upon the stage, but, of course, there was no career in reading in public forty years ago any more than there is to-day. He had a good stage presence and a pleasant voice, with no particular 'local colour' in his pronunciation, and a good broad, robust style of delivery . . . His programme in the Ulster Hall included many of the pieces familiar to students of one of the 'elocutions' of the mid-nineteenth century, and he spoke them in the best class-room manner, without affectation or unduly striving after effect. I was also present when he acted in *Richelieu*, and also in *Othello*. He had accepted the lead of Barry Sullivan in both characters, and that was the popular one of his day.

Only Sullivan, for all his tricks of intonation, running up the scale in some lines and down to the deepest depths in others, had a stage gait that gave one a sense of command so necessary in the part of the Cardinal, as well as that of the Moor; and I do not think that Mayne was sufficiently sure of himself to be able to affect this easily. There is really nothing absurd in comparing an amateur like Mayne with a veteran like Sullivan in such a part as *Richelieu* . . . *Othello* is quite another affair. The passion of the Moor is just too real for simulation . . . When Irving acted Othello with Edwin Booth as Iago, I am bound to say that I never witnessed a performance that seemed to me so unsatisfactory . . . Irving's incoherent ravings jarred upon me in the passionate scenes. He seemed no more than an extremely bad tempered man going from tantrum to tantrum. But his Iago to Booth's Othello was as fine a performance as I could wish to see. When Mayne was Othello his Iago was Robert B. Mantell, who spoke his lines as well as I ever heard them spoken. He made Iago a very gentlemanly person, and his cynical confessions when he found himself alone had the right touch of comedy about them.

. . . The two greatest living critics of the Shakespearian drama are closely associated with Belfast. Professor Boas[135] has been unwearied in his investigations, and Mr W. J. Lawrence[136] was the first to show us under what conditions the author of Shakespeare's plays . . . wrote and produced what he had written . . .

LII

Newspapers of Belfast • Pioneer Evening Papers
The Leaders of the Sixties

Having before me at the moment of writing the current number of the monthly magazine, *The Mercury*, I am reminded of the days of long ago, when, on going to my first school, the sole master of which was the Rev. Adam D. Glasgow, I passed daily the office of a *Mercury* newspaper. I never saw a copy of the paper, but I was an earnest student of the contents bill displayed in the window of the publishing office, which was situated in Arthur Street . . . I fancy that the paper had ceased publication before I had arrived at a paper-reading age. I never heard that particular organ mentioned by anyone in Belfast, and I am unable to say what political faith, if any, it professed . . . I do not know whether it was a weekly or a bi-weekly or a daily journal. I do remember very distinctly, however, another Belfast newspaper of a somewhat later date, which claimed a celestial origin, not of the planetary system, but of the stellar. This was the *Northern Star*. I have seen copies of this paper, but never beyond the hands of the boys who hung about Bridge Street and the entrance to Hercules Place. I believe that its patrons were to be found mostly in this unsavoury locality . . . through Smithfield and on to Peter's Hill and the Falls. I do not know when the *Northern Star* began to shine or when it set.[137] In those days the paper which seemed most popular was the *Morning News*. It professed to be 'independent' in its opinions. It was printed in Crown Entry, off High Street, and was accounted a good property. I think it became amalgamated with some other paper soon after the death of its proprietor; but this is comparatively recent history.[138]

In the sixties the recognised organ of the Conservative party was the *News-Letter* and that of the Liberals was *The Northern Whig*, each of which issued a weekly edition. But there was also a paper called *The Banner of Ulster*,[139] which had an office in Donegall Street. The early *News-Letter* was, I think, published in Bridge Street, and the *Whig* in Callender Street. The rivalry between the two latter was very pronounced, and the personalities indulged in by both were of a type that would astonish in the polite journalism of to-day. Mr Frank Finlay had taken over the *Whig* on the death of his father, and Mr James Alexander Henderson was proprietor of the *News-Letter*. I think it was in 1871 or 1872 that the *Whig* was removed to the Corn Exchange Buildings, and within a very short space it was sold to Sir John Arnott who had previously acquired the *Irish Times*. Mrs Frank Finlay was a daughter of Mr Russell, of *The Scotsman*, and she found the change from Edinburgh to Belfast too trying. In London, to which they migrated, she and her husband found themselves the centre of a congenial circle, which included artists, authors, and actors . . . Mr James Alexander Henderson was long one of the most distinguished of Belfast citizens. He was Mayor in 1874 and 1875, and his fine presence and courtly bearing . . . gained for him the esteem and admiration of his fellow-townsmen. His friendships were many and unvarying, and his family life was of the happiest type. Being in contact with him daily for several years I had come to regard him with affection as well as respect. His advice on all questions under consideration was invariably sound, and influenced by an unfailing kindliness.

Among my newspaper recollections is that of the flourish with which a new daily was announced in, I think, 1873. It was to be called *The Times* . . . I never heard who were the proprietors, but it was printed by Messrs D. & J. Allen. I do not recollect having seen a copy of this venture, and it cannot have languished for many months before it went to pieces 'unwept, unhonoured, and unsung'. Ten or twelve years later, if I remember rightly, another newspaper venture bounced into existence in Belfast. It was about the time when one of Mr Gladstone's Irish Land Acts was passed, when it was expected that every tenant in the country would appeal to have a fair rent fixed for his holding, and the new paper was to be the organ of the agricultural classes in Ulster. I recollect the initial number of this journal (the *Daily Post*). It had a leading article that ran well into three columns! The venture was engineered by a few amateurs who were under the impression that success in journalism . . . could be achieved without experience or a knowledge of the technique of a highly technical business.

. . . The *Belfast Evening Telegraph* was produced in 1870. For a town such as Belfast was even then to be without an evening paper must have seemed to many people to be amazing. Here a real 'long-felt want' was apparent, and there was a long experienced technical expert on the spot to supply it. All the qualifications to success were at hand, and when, on my way to the Bangor station, I bought a copy of the first number, I felt that its success was assured. Everyone in the train seemed to have bought a copy, and that evening marked the beginning of a new era in Belfast, when the evening paper in the train was looked on as being as necessary as a ticket. I could not help recalling that incident when I found myself one of the little company who were invited to give a technical opinion respecting a new morning paper that was being 'tried' in London in 1894 with the title of the *Daily Mail* . . . My verdict was: 'It has success stamped upon every column'; and that was what I felt when, more than 20 years earlier I bought my first copy of the *Belfast Evening Telegraph*. I was more fortunate in these predictions than I usually am when the role of prophet is forced upon me.

I have a very clear recollection of an attempt that was made to take advantage of Messrs Bairds' announcement that an evening paper was about to be published in Belfast . . . Before the *Evening Telegraph* had got well afloat there appeared the *Evening Press*. I bought a copy, and the first glance I had of its front page made me certain of its doom. I remember what a forbidding look there was about the heavy capitals in which the name was set up. The type was . . . far too heavy for any newspaper not exclusively designed for obituary notices. I never saw a second copy, though I suppose it must have spread its gloom through certain circles for a few months . . .

LIII

Two Remarkable Careers Start in Donegall Street One Ends as Chief Justice • Bullet Terminates Other

Fifty years ago the names of John Rea and Joe Biggar were intimately connected with Belfast . . . John Rea was a solicitor of not more than the ordinary ability essential to success in a police court practitioner . . . He hungered after notoriety, apparently without caring what form it assumed. I had many proofs of his disregard of the possibility of getting other people into trouble in his endeavours to force himself into the limelight of publicity. A contemporary of his in the same profession was located in the same street – Donegall Street, in his early days. He was the Charles Russell who became Lord Russell of Killowen and Lord Chief Justice of England[140] . . . his success embittered the latter part of Rea's life until he put an end to it with a revolver bullet . . .

I think that [Rea]'s earliest bid for notoriety was upon the occasion of the hearing of a Belfast Corporation Bill in a committee room of the House of Commons, and this must have been in 1862 or 1863 . . . I believe that he refused to retire, and had to be forcibly removed. 'Scenes' within the precincts of Westminster were unknown in those days . . . and John Rea seemed to feel that he had found out what role in life suited him best, and forthwith set about the business of scene-maker . . . He was a fluent public speaker, and his grammar was never at fault, no matter how excited he might become; but in no sense was he an orator. He had half-a-dozen phrases which made some people laugh, but they were meaningless phrases – one . . . was an allusion to what he called 'ace-of-hearts Whigs'. What that was supposed to mean no one could say, but he reiterated it ad nauseam, and when he got his laugh he seemed proud. He had a rooted animosity to some prominent people in the town, and his references to them were of the coarsest description. During the latter years of his life I used to see him occasionally in the theatre. He would put himself into a prominent position before the rise of the curtain, and when someone in the gallery recognised him, and began stamping on the hollow boards, he would come forward and solemnly 'take the salute'. His vogue as an advocate dwindled away in the seventies . . . He shot himself at his house in Donegall Street in 1882.[141]

Having mentioned ... Lord Russell of Killowen, I may say that I met two or three persons in Belfast who remembered him when he had an office as solicitor in Donegall Street. One of these gentlemen assured me that he had coached Russell as to the 'points' of a speech he was to make on some political subject, and the same gentleman gave me to understand that young Russell was inclined to be timid in public. It struck me that he contrived to overcome this particular failing in the course of time ...

Joseph Gillies Biggar ... was a member of a highly-respected family in Belfast. His father was a quiet retiring gentleman, and his sister, with whom I was acquainted, was a lady who devoted her life to the welfare of others. They were both of a retiring nature, and their home life, even with Joe as a third, was of the happiest type. But Joe was gifted (if that is the right word) with a saturnine form of humour, which he exercised upon every occasion. He was a shrewd, cynical tradesman, whom experience of humanity had led not to be so confiding in his fellow man as to trust them when he had not his eye on them. He seemed to me to have taken as a model Shakespeare's Duke of Gloster, whom he resembled physically. Gloster was the last man who would be likely to be successful as a lover, but he was un-doubtedly successful, and Joe Biggar set himself out to suggest the plausibility of Shakespeare's creation of Richard.[142] This ambition of his eventually led to his temporary undoing, but what was tragedy with Parnell, was with 'Joe' little beyond grotesque comedy. 'What is your profession?' he was asked when in the witness-box. 'A pig-jobber', replied Joseph; and he knew that that reply had reduced by a couple of hundred pounds the compensation awarded by the jury to that Miss Hyland whom he had promised to marry. His raucous voice cut that silken thread of romance that ran, if somewhat askew, through the law-court story of the Irish exile's sojourn in Paris. What compensation should be awarded to a damsel who has been jilted by a jobber in pigs? I believe that the assessment of the jury was something like £200; and Joseph Gillies smiled that knowing smile that was all his own; it was the facial equivalent of his staccato Earl Street accent.[143]

But Miss Hyland's action for his breach of promise only came toward the close of his public career. He had many adventures in the years between his candidature for a seat at the Water Board and his Hyland fling. He got returned to Parliament in the Home Rule interest, and before long he had distinguished himself in the House ... It was he who fooled the Speaker and the House of Commons by making what was alleged to be a 'speech' of many hours duration, involving the reading of many pages of irrelevant Blue books ... He was undoubtedly the Puck of Parliament for session after session. But he was of some value to his party, for at that time the Home Rulers included men compared with whom a pig-jobber was a sort of merchant prince, and the funds of the party were low. The trouble was to find a man possessing the credit and qualifications necessary for a treasurer, and Joe was appointed paymaster of the phalanx. I believe that he discharged his duties admirably ... Certainly Joseph Gillies Biggar had his uses, and for myself I never heard an unkind word spoken of him.

LIV

Belfastman on Woolsack • *Father Butler at Lisburn*
£10,000 Breach Recalled • *Electors of the Sixties*

Having written something about that most distinguished Lord Chief Justice of England, who had early associations with Belfast, but who I had never seen in my young days, I feel that I am more

than justified in touching upon the local connections of the distinguished Lord High Chancellor, whom I saw at a respectful distance
more than once during my schooldays. This was, of course, Hugh
M'Calmont Cairns,[144] who was for several years one of the two
representatives of Belfast, and who was knighted on becoming
Attorney-General in Disraeli's first government, and whose next
move was to the woolsack with the usual earldom. I remember very
distinctly seeing him by the side of the second candidate crossing
from the Northern Bank to his committee rooms in the Victoria
Hall; but I am unable to say whether his companion was Mr
Samuel Gibson Getty or that Mr Davison who was for some time
the second Conservative member for the borough. My recollection
of the appearance of Mr Cairns and the way he raised his hat in
acknowledging the little cheer that greeted him, is as vivid to-day
as if the incident had happened yesterday. He was a tall, intellectual
looking man, with a very slight stoop . . . Assuredly Earl Cairns never
forgot the position in which his ability had placed him. I am not
quite sure whether it was his father or his grandfather who had been
butler in some house in the neighbourhood of Lisburn. But Mr
Labouchere took occasion to refer to the genealogy of the Earl when
commenting in *Truth* upon the action for breach of promise which
a Miss Finney, the daughter of a London coal dealer, was bringing
against Lord Garmoyle, the eldest son of Earl Cairns.[145] . . .

As soon as Earl Cairns had got all that he could possibly have
looked for out of Belfast the town knew him no more . . . So long as
I remained in the North I never heard of his visiting it, nor did I
ever hear his name mentioned by anyone . . . [146]

The general elections of the pre-ballot days were infinitely
more exciting than those of to-day . . . the polling went on for
several days and the numbers were posted up practically every
hour; but this was not done by any official returning officer, so that
the agents of the various candidates were free to make public

whatever figures they pleased. Now and again, too, the electors
were assured that one of the candidates had retired, and the advice
was given to 'plump' for one of those who remained in the running.
The official announcement of the result of the poll took place at
hustings outside the Courthouse on the Crumlin Road. The most
exciting contest that I remember was when Mr William Johnston,
of Ballykilbeg, was returned after his incarceration for his infringe-
ment of the Party Processions Act . . . there was rarely any more
definite questions than that of Liberalism and Conservatism, until
Mr Gladstone's Disestablishment of the Church Bill was under
consideration. This was in 1869.

It was in the year before that Thomas M'Clure, the Liberal
candidate, was returned. He was an amiable old gentleman, who was
liked by everyone, as most persons of that type are. His claim to universal admiration seemed to lie in his excellent digestion, and his
grey hat of the old beaver pattern. The stories that were circulated
by his admirers respecting his trencher feats were awe-inspiring.
One spoke with bated breath of his having ordered two legs of
mutton to meet the immediate requirements of himself and one
guest, and how, though the guest failed to appear, both legs of
mutton disappeared. That was a schoolboy tale that I recollect, but
whether it came from the Liberal or the Conservative side I never
found out. He was wise enough never to open his mouth – unless in
the dining-rooms – of the House of Commons; but to be punctual
in his attendance, and to follow his leader into the right lobby on a
division . . . In an autograph letter Mr Gladstone informed him
that her Majesty had made up her mind to beg his acceptance of a
baronetcy. He could not see his way to decline the honour, so he
became Sir Thomas M'Clure, Bart . . . he retired from Parliament,
and took a wife to himself. I fancy he was then only a year or two
past seventy; but the lady was not of the traditional eighteen. The
union was a very happy one until the death of Sir Thomas a

considerable time later. He was one of the most popular citizens, and I am sure that he was incapable of offending anyone.[147]

One of the candidates at the election in the autumn of 1868 was Mr John Mulholland, and I fancy that Sir Charles Lanyon was another; but I was more interested in cricket than candidates in those days, and I do not think I knew who was returned to the House of Commons. I believe that Sir Charles Lanyon had received his knighthood the previous year; but Mr Mulholland did not become Lord Dunleath until some time later. He had inherited the great 'Mulholland's Mill', which broadened out in the form of the York Street Spinning Company, Limited.[148]

To those of us who became aware of the enormous issues on which the Home Rule elections were fought, the motives and contests of the sixties seem trivial . . . They had a different aspect to the two rival parties, for during the polling hundreds of extra police were drafted into the town to keep the peace, and some of the streets were lined with military . . . Sabres were flashing, and bayonets twinkling on every side . . . a full dress election, or even one conducted in demi-toilette, was very exhilarating to schoolboys . . .

LV

*The Days of My Youth • R.A. Institution of Sixties
Great Teacher of English • Old Pupil's Warm Tribute*

When I first went to the Royal Academical Institution it was still referred to . . . as the Old College. The New College was, of course, the Belfast Queen's College of the University of Ireland, and it was frequently alluded to by the older generation as such. The head-masters were – of the English School, Mr Carlisle; of the Classical, Dr Steen; of the Mathematical; the Rev. Isaiah Steen; of the French, Mr J. J. Wilde; of the Drawing, Mr Molloy; and of the Writing, Mr John H. Howell . . . It was open for a boy to attend one school only, each being charged separately. There was limited accommodation for boarders, divided equally between Mr Carlisle and Dr Steen. Only two of the masters had nicknames; the Rev. Isaiah was known as ' Taties', and Dr Blaine as 'Timmy'. The younger Steen was known as 'the Doctor'. He had a PhD degree from some German University. A former writing master was, I believe, a Mr Shealds, and the boys who had suffered under him referred to him as 'Paddy'. I was booked for the English, Mathematical, and Writing only, for some time; then I dropped the Writing for the Classical Department, at which I rejoiced.

Mr Carlisle's predecessor was Dr Thomas Blaine, but after retiring from the headmastership he retained his connection with the English school by having a classroom for the study of what was called belles-lettres, and I was fortunate enough to stray into this room within an hour of my passing through the open portals of the old Institution, and I can safely say that I have never left that room since. The difference between Dr Blaine and the other masters was . . . the difference between Shakespeare and Southey. The first words that I heard on entering the English school came from Mr Carlisle. 'Gentlemen, you're conversing', was his sharp reproof that arrested the chatter for a few moments while he entered the names of the new boys. When I sneaked into the classroom beyond, the words that greeted me were 'Hail, holy Light', beginning the sublime apostrophe in *Paradise Lost*. On a horsehair chair between the two long tables with the benches on either side sat a little white-haired man speaking in a truly reverential way Milton's matchless verse. He went on to the end of the passage, and he was interrupted by no whisper . . . I had an impression of having entered a new world – a world of wonder with an atmosphere of mystery . . .

It was not that I had the least literary learning. I had none that I was aware of up to that moment. I had read plentifully, but I had never been aware of the existence of literature in all my reading. But before Dr Blaine had come to the end of that page of Milton I had the impression of standing on the threshold of 'some dark shore, just seen that it was rich'.

I have talked with many men who sat in that classroom, and among them there was not one who did not speak of that old man with the deepest affection . . . I do not hesitate in expressing the opinion that no saner judgment on every question connected with literature, whether in the form of poetry or prose, than that which came from him, was ever given to the world by even the most highly esteemed of critics. He had a delicacy of perception that impressed the most reckless of us and gave us something to think about . . . But for his guidance we might have missed our way among the straggling walks of literature. He saw clearly what we only saw as in a glass darkly, and unlike most of the professors whom I have met, he was not content merely to give us his opinion . . . ; if we had a doubt – and he was ever ready to hear us express our doubts – he would not rest until he had convinced us that his opinion was correct. He daily made us aware of the derivation of the word 'education', for assuredly he led us out of our foggy atmosphere to inhale the invigorating draughts of the heights to which Shakespeare and Milton had soared . . .

At his own expense he had printed scores of pamphlets containing the passages he had selected from the English poets. Some of Shakespeare's plays he had in full – his favourite was *Macbeth* – and many passages from *Paradise Lost*, *L'Allegro*, *Il Penseroso*, *Comus*, and *Samson Agonistes*. He had about twenty pages of Pope, of Byron, and quite as many of Scott, of Campbell, of Wordsworth and Whittier. He had all the Falstaff scenes of Shakespeare. We read them daily – one boy one line – for half an hour, and for another half hour he talked about the whole, analysing passage after passage, giving us the names of the figures of speech employed in each, and not hesitating to point out the errors of the best authors. He made us aware of Shakespeare's anachronisms, and the ridiculous blunders of Pope's Homer . . . I think he could repeat the Greek text from memory to the extent of many thousand lines, and he would only pull himself up when he had got through a few hundred, with a shrewd smile, shaking his head. 'I must not take the bread out of Dr Steen's mouth', he would say. When I . . . advanced to Dr Steen's school, which was upstairs, I had an inkling of all that smile meant. Dr Steen was a teaching machine. He was the most dispiriting of masters, for beyond the baldest interpretations of the Greek and Latin texts he never went . . . Dr Blaine could smile at his own suggestion that he was depriving 'the Doctor' of his due.

He had all the fastidiousness of a man who is a scholar at heart, not merely regarding scholarship as a profession, and no matter how frequently or how flagrantly a beautiful passage might be read by us, he was prepared to show us all there was in it . . . A few years ago, there was a correspondence in a literary journal respecting the accented syllable in 'Trafalgar'. Everyone knows that Byron laid the accent upon the last syllable; but in the generally accepted pronunciation it was on the mid-syllable – so it is in Braham's well-known song "'Twas in Trafalgar's Bay' . . . Dr Blaine . . . when we were reading 'Childe Harold' with him . . . told us that when people at home were talking about Nelson's victory off Cape Trafalgar, they placed the accent as Braham had done, but they found that the sailors who had been in the Fleet . . . referred to it as Byron did in his poem, which was in accordance with the Spanish pronunciation . . . But Dr Blaine would not make any excuse for Byron's

writing 'there let him lay'. Only last year there was published
Byron's own letter in reply to Hobhouse . . . 'Laziness, simply
laziness', wrote Byron in reply to his friend's objection to the 'lay'.
'I did not want to miss a post'. When I came upon this characteristic confession of the poet, I could not help wondering what our
dear old Dr Blaine would have said if we had tried to excuse a
blunder on the same ground.

Dr Blaine had many quaint touches of humour in the handling
of his class. Instead of blurting out 'wrong!' . . . he would shake his
head and gently smile when a boy made a wild reply to his question.
'I think, Master Brown, you are labouring under a mistake', was his
favourite phrase. The work of every morning was enlivened by
some of his quaint comments, all of which were of a genial and
good-natured type . . . Attendance here did not involve any home
preparation of a lesson. Nor did it necessitate the writing of so
many 'lines', but I am certain that more real education emanated
from its precincts than . . . the combined rooms of the other schools.
Some hours in every week were devoted to the 'memorising' of
passages from his little books . . . A year's sitting around the tables
in this room was sufficient to allow of our laying in a store of
classical verses that should suffice us for the rest of our lives . . . I
have never forgotten any of the thousands of lines which I studied
at that time; and I felt conscious of winning the respect of a young
woman of my own household the other day when I was able to
repeat a whole page from *Comus* which she was studying for one of
her examinations. I had not looked at that passage since I had been
at school more than fifty years before . . .

I feel that I have but inadequately expressed my sense of all that
I owe to this great master . . . I had an opportunity of referring to
Dr Blaine in the article I wrote at the request of my friend Mr T. P.
O'Connor, for the 'Days of my Youth' page in one of his news-
papers. I did not refer to him by name, but several of his past pupils

identified him . . . and warmly bore out my eulogy of his character
and attainments.

On his final retirement he went to live at Conlig, and when there
he was approached by Lord Dufferin to allow some members of his
family to read with him. Dr Blaine acquiesced, but only with the
stipulation that he should receive no salary. Lord Dufferin . . .
begged that Dr Blaine would allow him to have a magazine or
weekly paper sent to him from the publisher so long as he lived. Dr
Blaine chose the *Saturday Review*, which in those days was the
leading literary journal. I regret to say that in an early issue of this
paper he had to read a slashing criticism of my first volume of
verse. He called to offer me his sympathy; but when he found that
I was not quite broken down, he laid a kindly hand on my shoulder,
saying 'You'll do – yes, you'll do'.

And I did.

LVI

50 Years Ago at 'Inst' • *Gentleness of Dr Steen*
Father of the Driver Type • *Mayne Reid Under Cover*

It would be ridiculous in the extreme for me to offer any critical
remarks in regard to the teaching at the Royal Academical
Institution of fifty odd years ago. But I need hardly say that fifty
odd years ago I never hesitated doing both . . . We were always
ready to express with the utmost frankness our opinion regarding
the school and its staff . . . It was understood that a cane was in

repose in a press in some room on the ground floor, but . . . so long as I was at the old institution I never saw that rod or heard its swish. Upon one occasion I remember a rumour reached us in the English school that some one had been 'tipped' by 'The Doctor' . . . [but] whosoever might resort to the cane, [it] would not be 'the Doctor'.

We all knew 'beyond peradventure', as President Wilson would have put it, that Dr Steen was the mildest-mannered man that ever conjugated the Greek 'tupto'. I have often thought that if he had kept to that 'tupto' instead of being so ready to pass on to 'tuptomai', he would have had an easier time.[149] The general 'note' of the old institution was gentleness and gentlemanliness, and the leading exponent of both was assuredly Dr Steen. I never saw him without a copy of Xenophon's *Anabasis*, and I soon discovered that the treatise had become the text-book of his life; for he seemed to be ever on the retreat from the exasperating menaces of the young barbarians.[150] He should never have been a schoolmaster. His vocation was, I am sure, the ministry, as plainly as that the class-room rather than the pulpit was for his father, the Rev. Isaiah, who had been a minister, and still wore his white cravat, when giving us, with all the emphasis of his namesake when addressing the Israelites, his opinion of our indolence and predicting our down-fall. Doctor Steen was a gentle creature . . . I am certain that there was not one of us who had not an affection for him, or who did not feel (for a minute or so) some remorse for annoying him . . . To be in keeping with the best traditions of school stories, I should have been a careless young reptile like one of Mr Kipling's schoolboys.[151] But however humiliating it may be, I admit that I was a good boy in the classical school, and if I had my shins barked by the toes of my classmates, on that account, I did not grumble. I wore as trustworthy boots as the best of them, and I was sly. I kicked back without any unnecessary fuss or apology, and went on with my conjugations . . . Under such a master as Dr Steen one learned nothing beyond the rudiments of the great classics. One was not there to go any further than was necessary for matriculation at the university . . . His work was little beyond drudgery and I think he knew it. In spite of his easy-going and his placid nature, he broke down at a comparatively early age. His placidity became paralysis, and only the devotion of his wife made his last years endurable. I used to see him by her side walking painfully through the Botanic Gardens, but he failed to recognise me.

His father, the Rev. Isaiah Steen, was, as I have said, the principal of the mathematical school. He was the very antithesis of 'The Doctor'. His voice was like the butt of a ram, and he was untiring in his employment of it. To enter his class-room was like looking into a goods station at shunting time. He was conscientious to a fault, we thought; we felt that he might easily have spared himself – and us – but he did neither. His zeal was of that slow, steam-roller order which is effective in its own way. He was a drover, and he had need to be a drover, for mathematics have to be driven into the brains of most boys by sheer force. When one went into his school after spending a graceful hour with the best poets in Dr Blaine's company, one regarded Thompson's arithmetic as a vulgar fraction, and the problems of Euclid as adding insult to injury. But the Rev. Isaiah very soon showed us that though rhythm and arithmetic had the same parentage, yet the two had drifted apart through the stress of centuries, and if we did not speedily recognise this fact he would take it upon him to convince us of its bearing on our immediate future . . . His demonstration of the problem of how to pass satisfactorily an idle hour in his vicinity was of that reductio ad absurdum principle so dear to Euclid. 'To fancy that I am unable to see the difference between the crimson cover of *The Scalp Hunters*[152] and *Thompson's Arithmetic* would be to think that I am a fool, which would be absurd', was the equivalent to his formula, and it usually wound up the discussion, Q.E.D. He had a sense of his responsibility to the parents of the boys as well as to the honour of the school . . . He would have turned me out of the building if I had ventured to suggest . . . that the cultivation of the faculty for hoodwinking a master tends more to success in life than the ability to discover the exact value of a legendary and elusive X.

We had all something more than a sneaking regard for 'Taties', even after he had abused us soundly – almost as soundly as we deserved – winding up his vituperation with the assurance that we were robbing our parents if we insisted on neglecting to assimilate all the arithmetic for which they had paid their hard-earned money . . . I should know because he addressed it to myself – it was *The Headless Horseman* that he found enclosed between the brown leather back of an old Thompson . . . I was moved to tears upon that occasion, and I deny that their source was my mortification at having been found out. It took me forty odd years to discover a repartee to his accusation. I know now, when it is fortunately half a century too late, that I should have pointed out to him, firmly, but with discretion, that my trick of concealing my actual intention by what is now called camouflage embodied the medium by which every great commander became a hero – when successful. I might even have gone further and assured him that if it were not for resorting to the equivalent of my trick, more than half of the animal, vegetable, and stock exchange world would be annihilated. Unfortunately, however, the theory of evolution had not been more than hinted at in those days. Darwin was still pondering over the results of the voyage of the *Beagle*, and Mr Robert Patterson was quoting Milton as an 'authority' in his *Natural History for use of Schools*.

From the class-room of the Rev. Isaiah Steen, more than one Cambridge Wrangler has graduated . . . he laid the foundation for many a successful commercial career to which his mathematics contributed largely . . . Whatever mentality I may have possessed at one time I can safely say that it did not soar in any admired contemplation of figures . . .

Regarding the assistant masters in the mathematical or the classical schools I need not say much. They were invariably young men who hoped to graduate one day at Queen's College; but I do not think that any one of them had yet matriculated . . . In the Caesar or Virgil classes I fancy that the assistants were only about a week ahead of the boys. That was, however, enough for practical purposes, provided that they maintained their lead. There was one who, I think, fell a day or two behind, and that was a little embarrassing . . . At the Old Institution I am sure it would have been thought very much infra dig for one of the assistants to have appeared on the playground without his coat. I only recollect the Doctor stopping for a few minutes on his way to his own side of the building when a match was being played. He removed his spectacles, polished the lenses and went on wondering what it was all about – a benevolent 'boys-will-be-boys' expression upon his face.

LVII

Father of Lady Pirrie • Smile a Family Heritage
R. A. Institution Memories • Shorthand 'Feat' of Sixties

Mr John Carlisle was the principal of the English school who succeeded Dr Blaine. He was a tall good-looking man, whose features never lost their smile even when the stress of circumstances seemed to compel a contrary expression. I learned that that smile was a family possession, and in course of time I had sufficient data to enable me to trace it from one branch of the family to another. It was at all times natural, and, consequently, pleasing. It took away from that enforced sternness which was supposed to give dignity to schoolmasters and county court judges and policemen. Mr Carlisle never seemed trying to assert his dignity, but he never seemed to us otherwise than dignified, with the bearing of a genial and considerate gentleman . . . He treated us and addressed us as gentlemen – I have already said that the first words I heard from him were 'Gentlemen, you're conversing' – and I am convinced that most of us who had no irresistible impulses towards 'gentle-manliness' made a distinct advance in that direction under the benign influence of the headmaster. I never knew of his losing his temper for a moment . . .

There was no mechanical discipline in the English school under Mr Carlisle . . . We were not marched or counter-marched into our places; we were given a reasonable time to settle down after a change from one school to another . . . We were allowed to converse while we were on the floor, but when we settled down, three at a desk, we were expected to be silent in regard to our own affairs and to attend to our work . . . At the close of each lesson vouchers of merit were distributed . . . If a boy got through without losing a mark he had a ticket; but a single mistake was sufficient to disqualify. Forty-eight of those tickets represented a shilling book to be purchased at Mullan's, and this was something quite independent of the usual examination prizes distributed at the end of the term. This system, which applied only to the English school, was discontinued before I left the Institution.

The school books were very elementary. The grammar was of the commonplace type of the old Lindley Murray, without any of the modern etymology in respect of the construction of sentences and the like, and the geography volume was of the most rudimentary type . . . There were a huge pair of revolving orbs in the room, one of which every now and again was wheeled on its castors in front of a class and we were initiated into the mysteries of latitude and longitude, by the aid of a flexible sector, applied to the governing frame-work. The demonstration was wholly confined to the terrestrial globe; the celestial remained in a dusty corner . . .

The English history was that excellent one compiled by Dr W. F. Collier, who at that time was head of a school in Glasgow or Edinburgh, and who some years afterwards became principal of the Belfast Academy . . . Mr Carlisle did not take up the attitude of the captain of a vessel who leaves the navigation in the charge of his mates, and only appears with his sextant to work out the day's run; he invariably took one of the classes in person . . . not only was he enabled to become personally acquainted with the character and attainments of the boys, but he enabled the boys to take his measure . . . So far from the news of Mr Carlisle's intention to take a particular class causing any trepidation . . . it was regarded as a compliment . . . He was no hustler – the word had not been invented then . . . but his attitude was one of encouragement and persuasion. When one of us made an unusually glaring mistake he would look disappointed and pained, and he was always ready to give one a chance of revising one's answer to his question. . . .

The only trouble was that the finished courtesy of the principal made the crudities of the underlings more apparent and unen-durable . . . However ineffectual the various Educational Acts have been . . . if they have failed to make good scholars they have cer-tainly made accomplished teachers. In the days of my youth anyone who had failed in any other line of business was reckoned good enough to be a teacher of English. Mr Carlisle's assistants were probably as competent as might be found in other schools in England as well as in Ireland. I believe that the building of the Methodist College brought about a considerable change in this respect so far as Belfast was concerned. Some of the assistant-masters under Dr Parker were men of high scholastic achievements; more than one of them had edited classical textbooks and all of them were professional teachers, and were not merely in the novitiate stage of entering the class-room while qualifying for other professions. I recollect that one of Mr Carlisle's assistants got a job in the General Post Office of a character that made few demands upon his scholarship beyond the counting of change and the registering of parcels. But I do not believe that the most highly qualified of the three or four could have passed the pretty stiff examination necessary for such an appointment to-day. The personality of the principals at the R.A.I. was, however, great enough to be paramount as an educational factor, and so there was little reason for complaint in the long run.

The writing department was an adjunct of the English, and the master was a genial gentleman named Howell. The 'copperplate' was the standard set up; and legibility was supposed to be the sole aim of penmanship. There was no talk of 'current hand' or 'commercial hand' in those days. It was taken for granted that a boy would form his own style in accordance with the conditions of whatever his future occupation might be, and I am inclined to think that the handwriting of the majority of the pupils was as good as the average of the next generation, who were taught to run off a line without lifting the pen . . . Shorthand could be acquired at the same school . . . Mr Howell had an assistant who . . . could honestly lay claim to writing his thirty words a minute! Such a feat was thought . . . almost to border on the miraculous, for many years had to elapse before the young lady clerk appeared upon the scene, doing her 150 words from dictation . . .

Of the remaining masters of the Old Institution I am unable to write, for I did not come in contact with either Mr Wilde or Mr Molloy. The former taught French and German; but both these languages were spoken at my own home, and the art which the latter professed was considered an unnecessary accomplishment. Mr Wilde was appointed on the staff of the *Challenger* expedition . . . we found that he had unsuspected attainments as a naturalist, and that Professor Wyville Thompson had recommended his inclusion among the band of savants who sailed on that memorable voyage, the complete results of which have not even yet been made known to the world . . .

LVIII

Boys of the Old Brigade • Instonians of the Sixties
Fight at Bog Meadows • Late R. J. M'Mordie Held in Awe

Sitting down to write about my old schoolfellows at the Royal Academical, I seem to hear once again the strains of that marching song, 'Where are the Boys of the Old Brigade?' . . . There are some still, I am happy to think, in the land of the living. The others I salute in memory. I had never an angry moment with one of them, living or dead . . .

In the English school my desk mates were F. L. Heyn and Abram Combe. The latter left us for Rugby. We played our ball game with two wooden bats together during each of the two recesses, and cricket on Saturdays. They were the best mannered boys in the school. They were gentle and manly, and the combination of these qualities made me understand what Mr Carlisle meant when he said: 'Gentlemen, you're conversing' . . . At the desk next to ours there sat two brothers named Moran, the sons of a clergyman at Belmont. John, the elder, was a good-looking and clever boy. He went with many others, into a linen firm, but after a year or two he entered at the Queen's College, and, I think, he had his first degrees in arts; but of this I am not quite sure. He took part in the amateur theatricals which I got up with Joe Plunkett in aid of a hospital. He wrote some excellent poetry under the influence of Swinburne – verses as far beyond the current 'poets' corner' stuff in technique as Swinburne was beyond Tupper.[153] He never succeeded in getting a line published, and I think he became something of a trial to his family – a way that poets have when such mundane matters as a livelihood come forward for consideration. I heard that he eventually went to the United States where he died at an early age.

Herbert Chipp, whose name I have already mentioned, was also in our class. He was the son of the great organist and composer, and his metier was painting. He was an accomplished artist and his incomparable charm as a boy never left him . . .

Two others who sat close to us were Joe and Wallis Mackay, whose father was the Rev. Dr Mackay, the well-known Methodist clergyman, who for many years was the head of the Methodist College. The elder of the two brothers was something of an artist, but it was Wallis whose work on some London journals attracted a deal of attention. He was the original 'Captious Critic' of the old *Sporting and Dramatic*, and two or three of his drawings appeared in *Punch*. Tom Taylor was then its most incompetent editor, and he was by no means favourably disposed to the work of anyone who had referred to his plays except in flattering terms, and he never gave Wallis a chance after his first criticism as the 'captious'.[154] Wallis had humour, and if he had had a chance of a proper training he might have gained some distinction. He made a most unhappy marriage, and his death was a great blow to his many friends. No man in the Bohemian world of those days was a greater favourite

than poor Wallis. His brother Joe did some casual journalism in
London, and wrote a play which was taken on a provincial tour by
Kate Lawler, and Barry Sullivan got from him at least two acts of
another which was to be called *The Prodigal Son*. I heard that the
censor put his veto to the production, but I know that the author
laid the blame upon the actor.

I cannot remember the names of any others in our class who
excelled in the arts; but among those who were cut off before they had
a chance of doing anything definite in the world was a boy named
John Lavons. He was one of Dr Blaine's foremost pupils, having been
at the Institution when he was principal. Charlie Wetherall was one
of our little band who aimed at being thought 'select' . . . He was
the son of a military officer who held a high command in Belfast.
He was a cheery companion, wholly devoid of 'side'. As a matter of
fact, there were very few boys in my time who showed any tendency
to give themselves an air of superiority to the others in the same class,
after they had been in harness for a month . . . There were a few boys
who were regarded as 'outsiders', but they did not come aggres-
sively 'between the wind and our nobility', and one of them at least
became literally an 'outsider', being ordered out of the classroom
by Dr Carlisle with the breathless approval of the whole room . . .

One of the cleverest of our intimates was Drummond Porter, a
son of the Rev. John Scott Porter . . . When I made my first voyage
to the Cape I was greeted at the Custom House by one of the Porters,
and felt myself at home, especially as there was hanging on the wall a
fine photograph of the approaches to Belfast Lough.[155] Drummond
Porter's eldest brother had left the Institution before our day starting
on his career at the Bar which made him Master of the Rolls.[156]
Drummond and I kept in touch for over thirty years. Only once had
we a serious difference of opinion, and that was when I had called
Verdi vulgar . . . Willie Brown, a son of Mr John Shaw Brown, of
Edenderry, invariably sat beside me in Dr Blaine's class, and on the

other side was Douglas Ferguson, whose father was a professor at the Queen's. There were three Gillilands – Tom, Harry, and Jack. The last-named won an open scholarship at Cambridge, and got a good appointment in Calcutta. The two Ferrars who were in the same class belonged to a well-known Belfast family. Of their brothers one was a Fellow of Trinity College, Dublin, and another held an Indian judgeship, while Augustus was associated with the Jaffes in their great linen house. Henry was the elder of my contemporaries, but he left the Institution and spent a year at the Moravian school at Neuwied, on the Rhine. The younger married Miss Hartley, and after some years in the Ulster Bank went to Johannesburg to a banking house there . . .

In the Mathematical school I remember that the biggest boy was Robert McMordie, whose statue I saw with admiration when I was last in Belfast.[157] We all stood in great awe of him, and I think the Rev. Isaiah did also. At his desk any approach to levity was promptly blocked. I never met anyone who took life so seriously, unless it was his brother who was the doctor. It was a relief to find Robert McMordie's son playing heartily in a croquet tournament at Lewes some years ago, and treating the match with some measure of frivolity . . . Frank Hudson, who was beside me in the same school, went into the Indian Civil Service, and Joe Pike, I believe, found his mathematical training to stand him in good stead when he became an insurance agent in the town. I regretted to hear of his death some years ago.

In the classical school my intimates were Edwin Hughes, who graduated at the Queen's, and became a solicitor; Fred Spiller, whose death last year I deplored, and a handsome boy named Alec M'Cosh, a son of the well-known Dr M'Cosh.[158] Then there were two brothers of another professor, Sam and John Rogers, and the youngest son of Professor Andrews, the vice-president of the Queen's.[159] He was by far the best Greek scholar among us . . .

The great and memorable incident of the mid-sixties was the boxing match for the championship of the school, which took place at the Bog Meadows, and convulsed the whole community for some weeks . . . I remember the names of the two aspirants in our midst, one was Tom and the other was not Jerry, but Bob. I cannot understand how it was that the affair was allowed to come to a head by the authorities. For weeks beforehand nothing was talked about within the precincts but the coming fight, and every master must have been aware of what was on foot, and yet no active steps were taken to put a stop to it . . . On the day in March when the fight was to take place, the business of the school was to all intents and purposes, suspended, and at least a hundred of the boys marched to the meadows, where the ring was formed and seconds appointed, with sponges and towels. I believe that there was actually a scrimmage of some sort between Tom and Bob; but I saw nothing of it . . . The official result was the expelling of the two champions and their seconds, and the rustication of some of their supporters. That fight was the only scandal ever associated with the good name of the Royal Academical Institution, and I do not think it was a very serious one.

LIX

'Murdering' Cleopatra and Wrecking her Barge
The Stage in Belfast • Denunciatory Days and Now

The history of the Belfast stage has yet to be written. There was a time when it was reckoned almost on the level with Dublin in regard to the drama, and several of the great actors of the eighteenth and the early nineteenth century included the Ulster capital in their itinerary . . . I know nothing of the vicissitudes of the Belfast stage previous to the tenancy of the theatre in Arthur Square by Mr J. F. Warden, but I know that the tidal wave of prejudice against theatre-going in the town during the gloomy mid-Victorian era threatened to become a veritable deluge . . . To Mr J. F. Warden the credit is due of having so raised the tone of the local theatre that most of the prejudices which remained . . . were removed . . . In my young days there was not a clergyman belonging to any denomination in Belfast who had ever entered a theatre . . . every year an earnest churchgoer might count upon hearing at least one sermon devoted to the denunciation of theatres and theatre-going. I remember hearing one in the course of which the parson showed [such] a surprising knowledge of the technique of the profession as made at least one of his congregation feel that he had gained his information on the spot. At any rate, he was aware of the structural situation of the pit . . . allocating to it a position identical with that pit which was reputed to be bottomless. An attendance at the one, we were assured, would inevitably mean an eternity to be spent in the other.[160]

And Belfast did not stand alone in respect of the attitude of the majority of the inhabitants toward the stage . . . The Rev. Canon Hannay, whose boyhood was spent in Belfast, was certainly never taken to the theatre by his father, and yet he wrote without reproach to his cloth one of the most amusing comedies of its year.[161]

It is generally understood that the great change in the attitude of the Church in regard to the stage was due to Henry Irving and the Lyceum management. It was assumed that nothing that could offend the most sensitive ear would ever be heard on the stage of that theatre; and people began to talk of 'the great educational value of the theatre', and gradually the co-operation of the Church was obtained for dramatic performances . . . People were expected

In Belfast by the Sea

to go to the Lyceum in a properly devotional spirit, and to come away edified, and I am pretty sure that they were edified if Shakespeare was being represented.

It took some time, however, for Belfast to assimilate the new spirit of the age, and in the meantime Mr Warden had a pretty hard fight; but he lived long enough to witness and profit by the change in the attitude of all sections of the community respecting his enterprise. It was very early in the sixties that he became lessee of the Theatre Royal. Every provincial theatre in those days had its stock company, and Mr Warden's was, I believe, quite as good as might be found in any town in the kingdom, with the exception perhaps of Edinburgh or Manchester. Warden himself was a fine actor, both as regard tragedy and comedy. I never saw a better Sir Anthony Absolute[162] or Old Hardcastle;[163] and his wife, who had been Jenny Bellair, was a handsome woman, who took the boy's part in pantomime, singing and dancing admirably, year after year. In one of the earliest stock companies Edward Terry[164] was the low comedian, and a little later, after Terry had made his mark with John Hollingshead at the London Gaiety, Sam Johnson, who only left Belfast to join the Lyceum Company, acting all the low comedy parts in the repertoire of Irving. He was the best of the many gravediggers in *Hamlet* and by far the best Dogberry on the stage since Henry Compton. But generally the acting of 'the good old stock companies', as we sometimes hear them called by veterans, was wooden . . . When an actor had to study ten or twelve parts every week he probably became an adept in memorising, though I must say that I never heard of one who was letter perfect in any play of importance. But when the London companies came in their full strength on tour, or even when there was a provincial touring company formed for any special play, the local audiences were apt to talk slightingly of the stock actors and actresses.

The demobilisation of the Belfast company took place in 1880 or thereabouts. Previously the 'stars' in their courses came to Belfast trusting wholly to local support on the stage, no matter what the play might be. To be sure a few of the greatest took the precaution of bringing with them a leading man or leading lady as the case might be, but even so great a favourite as Barry Sullivan did not bring his Lady Macbeth with him or his Pauline. He had, however, a henchman named Cathcart who appeared as his Richmond and MacDuff, to withstand his fencing onslaughts . . . At first Miss Wallis travelled alone, but late in the seventies she brought her leading man with her, the first being Edward Compton, and the next Robert B. Mantell. Finally she travelled with a full company, but I do not think that Barry Sullivan ever did so.

. . . One went to the theatre to witness the representation of one character by a competent person and of a dozen by as many incompetents. The word 'support' was a favourite on the bills referring to the stock company, but they really did not support him; they let him down in every scene.

I remember the shock I had on one of my earliest visits to the old theatre to witness *Antony and Cleopatra*. I did not feel anything to be especially disillusioning until that marvellous passage was reached descriptive of the barge and its company – certainly the most wonderful lines in the whole of literature. The passage remained in my eyes as the recollection of one of those glorious early Italian pictures – full of colour and with a riot of exquisite detail dazzling the eyes. I waited breathlessly to hear the words spoken . . . while the actor was stumbling over the second line – it sounded in my ears as though he were describing a dog fight – he pronounced 'poop' as though it were spelt 'pup' – 'the pup was beaten . . .'

I turned away in silent but burning indignation; and yet when the fellow had finished he got a round of applause. That was my second blow. The public of the pit did not know which was bad from what was good. I soon . . . became cynical enough to join ironically in the plaudits of the puerile. Often . . . when I hear veterans talking of the good old days of the stock companies, with their marvellous feats of twelve parts a week, I have thought of . . . the 'juvenile lead' who wrecked Cleopatra's barge, and sent its timbers flying in spluttering splinters across the footlights.

LX

On the Stage and Off • 'Ah, My Heart is Weary Waiting' Pub as Life's Ambition • The Sixties in Belfast

I never heard of any members of our old stock companies achieving eminence in 'the profession' . . . I could never appreciate the force of that glamour of the footlights which caused many young women, who might have attained permanent distinction as cooks, to submit to the most meagre of living wages, and the squalor of lodgings in a back street, with the perpetual worry of new parts of the most rubbishy order . . . In Warden's companies the ambition of the leading gentleman, after some years of hard intellectual work, was usually turned toward the acquiring of a seven-day licence in a snug little public-house, and it is satisfactory to remember that some of them realised that position before growing too old . . .

When no 'stars' had been booked the bill was carried out by all who were 'on the strength'. There were dozens of melodramas and farces available for such occasions, and in the course of a season the public were privileged to become acquainted with a wide range of both. The dramas were not wholly ridiculous; the villains were deeply dyed, and the virtuous heroines were of the most Puritan strictness. The farces were mostly those which a man named Maddison Morrison was turning out by the dozen and selling for five pounds each – a reduction for three and seven counting as six . . . *Box and Cox* was of this type, and *Boots at the Swan*, as well as *A Cup of Tea* and *Woodcock's Little Game*. Nearly all were adapted from the French . . . Tom Taylor was the most prolific of English adaptors, but he never took the trouble to state on a play-bill the source of his four acts. I remember that the critic of the *Athenaeum* ventured to do so for him . . . [165] Mr Taylor was greatly annoyed, for there was no man who was more careful of his own rights, or who so insisted on every word in his precious dialogue being spoken as he had written it; but no action for libel followed. Even Tom Robertson's *Caste*, *School* and *Ours* . . . delightfully simple and natural plays, were not wholly original . . .

The most exciting of the stock pieces of the old theatre was, I think, *The Streets of London*.[166] It included enough crimes or attempted crimes to provide material for half a dozen melodramas. An effort at suicide by inhaling the fumes of burning charcoal was frustrated by a deeply persecuted but genial hero who happened to be in the next room – these heroes of the melodrama are so good-natured that they will do anything to oblige an author – and . . . the virtuous young man, and the even more virtuous young woman in virginal muslin, attained that happiness which in these adventures keeps dogging the virtuous, but invariably a minute or two too late to get in touch with them, until the last scene of the last act. I remember how well the part of the hero was played by Mr Harry Hampton, Warden's leading man for a season or two. I think he got a good part in a London company eventually.

The old theatre where such treats were obtainable on Saturday nights was a dingy and dilapidated building in the sixties. It had a large pit with rows of planks for seats without backs. The dress circle was upholstered in turkey red or what had once been turkey red, faded to a hue that was in perfect harmony with the general dinginess of the interior. The gallery was spacious and it had a resonant floor so that the applause of the gods became genuinely Olympian. Now and again a criticism of the acting or of a sentiment of the author came from above with all the force of a celestial evangel though not invariably in the language which might be thought consistent with such an origin. Now and again too the appearance of a local celebrity in the dress circle seemed to call for comment in the form of applause or hisses. I remember clearly the advice that was given from above to Barry Sullivan when in the battle scene in *Richard III* he rushed about thirsting for the blood of Richmond. It was in the year when people were talking about 'Liberty tints' and 'Art colours', and in order to show that he was quite up-to-date, Richard came on carrying a banneret of 'crushed strawberry' and 'peacock blue' which drooped in a triangular fashion over his shoulder.

From the opposite side of the stage there came on impetuously his antagonist, Richmond, and the two eyed one another viciously for a palpitating moment of silence. Then came a voice from the gallery: 'Clod away the wee parasol, Barry, and hoak the tripes out of him'. After a strenuous moment or two, Barry accepted the contract. He threw away the banner ... and getting close to the prompter in the wings, exchanged his ornamental sword for a more trust-worthy weapon of the cutlass order, [and] he hastened to attempt the delving operation suggested by his adviser in the gallery. That was a fight fierce enough to satisfy the most exacting, and if the pro-cess of evisceration was not carried out to the letter, it went far enough to convince the most sceptical that it was only left incomplete in order to satisfy the scruples of the author who pretended to claim historical accuracy for the incident of Bosworth Field.

The private boxes in the dingy old house were even more emphatically dingy than the faded fauteuils of the dress circle. They were literally boxes, square and lined with a cheap lodging-house wall-paper of a florid pattern. It was in one of these boxes that a group of officers of the garrison sat upon one occasion when G. V. Brooke, the great tragedian of mid-Victorian days, came on the stage in a condition that suggested to them that he was fully qualified to impersonate Cassio in his last scene – so much so that one of the party thought himself justified in delivering in collo-quial language the reproach of Othello.[167] The actor . . . addressed his suspected accuser in a way that was far from dignified, the imme-diate result being an unrehearsed scene between the stage and the box, followed by a challenge the next day . . . I believe there was a conference between the manager of the theatre and the commandant of the garrison, and an exchange of apologies was agreed on.

I am afraid there is more than a grain of truth in the old stories we used to hear of actors and inebriation. I heard from William Gilliland who, on leaving Belfast in 1876, became assistant managing editor on the London *Daily Telegraph*, and who was one of the most scrupulously accurate men I ever knew, that he had seen Brooke several times distinctly intoxicated on the stage . . . I think it may safely be assumed that such scenes have been obsolete for many years. For myself, I never saw an actor in action who was open to reproach in this connection . . .

Two actors of the good old warm-hearted school who came to the old theatre were John Coleman and Charles Dillon.[168] They were high-strung, emotional, and romantic persons, heaven-born interpreters of the grandiloquent heroes of Victor Hugo and the mercerised silk[169] heroes of Bulwer Lytton. Whatever may be said about them by highbrow critics . . . they never spared themselves;

they returned to their dressing-rooms after each act bathed in
perspiration . . . an actor had to work for a living like a navvy, and to
deliver his lines with a vehemence that almost blew out the gas in
the footlights. But the strong suit of those fine old fellows was the
ironic smile. It must have taken years to mature. But it was not safe
to take it out of doors. It made the horses shy. But with the rough
edges trimmed off the stereo before it became set, and lubricated
with the sardonic 'ha-ha!' it cannot but have struck terror into the
soul of the guilty baronet even though he was lurking with his
forged will behind a screen. Mr J. F. Warden founded his style upon
Charles Dillon in *Belphegor*, but he ran into none of the excesses of
his master . . .

LXI

*The Stage in Belfast • Sullivan and Irving
Barry's 'Hamlet' Comment • Salvini's 'Othello' Triumph*

It was to the oldest of the three theatres which I remember in
Belfast that the first provincial company came with Tom Robertson's
Caste, *School*, and *Ours* . . . after seeing these simple, natural trans-
criptions of home life with none of the tinsel sentiment or shoddy
heroics of Bulwer Lytton or Sheridan Knowles, theatre-goers began
to perceive that the stage might be employed for the presentation
of the real instead of the artificial . . .

The first touring company came to Belfast in 1870, Craven
Robertson, J. F. Younge, and Miss Brunton being among the most

competent of the cast . . . it was a company without a weak member, and the result . . . was to make theatre-goers . . . in the provinces generally very dissatisfied with the star system . . . The all-round perfection of which a sample had been brought before our eyes made us impatient at the shortcomings of the stock company, especially when emphasised by the ability of the star. Some years had passed, however, before the change came about, and meantime the old favourites coming in solitary state were welcomed as before. Of these the greatest in Belfast was Barry Sullivan.

This actor had made his reputation in London in all the 'heavy' parts in the repertory of the 'fifties and 'sixties, and he had introduced some new 'readings' of the text in *Hamlet* and *Macbeth*, most of which received the tribute of ridicule by students of Shakespeare. His 'I know a hawk from a heron, pshaw!' was one of the most notorious of his inventions . . . But Barry Sullivan did not create the enthusiasm with which he was greeted on account of any subtlety . . . He was in comparison with a real artist what a scene painter is to a miniaturist. He painted his characters in primary colouring and laid it on thick. But it must be said . . . that he spoke his words clearly, even when he was running up and down the scale as if to show the extent of his compass. In dealing with a complex character such as Hamlet he was beneath consideration, but in purely superficial parts such as Richelieu[170] or Alfred Evelyn[171] he was possibly as good as any actor of his day, and that was a day when most audiences were quite satisfied that Macbeth was wholly a murderous warrior, and Lady Macbeth his mate – cave-dwellers both. Sullivan ranted through scene after scene in the same strain as Macbeth and romped through scene after scene as Gloster, utterly oblivious of the terrific moments in each play, when the genius who created both characters shows the inmost soul of the man helpless in the contest with Destiny. When Irving played these parts he made us aware of what Sullivan lacked, but he also showed us that he lacked something which Sullivan had at his command. I was standing by Mr Warden ... when Irving appeared as Gloster, and when he came to the words that Sullivan used to deliver with a bellow that shook the house – 'Thou troublest me – I'm not i' the vein', and Irving spoke them with the sneer and leer of a Mephistopheles, I saw the manager looking in a dazed way around him. 'And they call that man an actor!' he whispered. A play that suited Sullivan in every way was that old specimen of the didactic drama *The Gamester*. The death scene was a sermon in very bad prose, lasting several minutes, although the particular poison that the wretched man swallowed would have killed an elephant in fifty seconds. The actor failed to impress anyone any more than a preacher does when he has been in the pulpit for over half an hour. He appeared as Charles Surface[172] as well as Claude Melnotte,[173] and was greatly admired in both parts.

Southern, who, in 1862, had been the Lord Dundreary of a play called *The American Cousin*,[174] came more than once to the old theatre ... and for charm his light comedy has never been surpassed. Charles Wyndham founded his style upon Southern, and approached him in lightness of touch and ingratiating finish, without a suspicion of any mannerism. For boisterous low comedy we had many visits from J. L. Toole. His best character was Paul Pry in *The Serious Family*, another adaptation from the French. The house roared over his Artful Dodger in a version of *Oliver Twist*, and in *Uncle Dick's Darling* we had some pathetic moments in a quavering falsetto. It was, however, in such farces as *Ici on Parle Français* that he was inimitable. But, of course, no play of this type could be witnessed with patience with any other actor in the part that Toole had made his own. He was a genial and amusing companion, and in his decrepit years, when he was wheeled on the stage of the Lyceum among Irving's guests on the first night of every play, he was a pathetic figure to those of us who remembered ... his merry days.

It was in 1872 that Warden built his second theatre . . . a great improvement upon the first. It was opened with an incomparable Italian Opera Company, including Madame Tietjens, Madame Sinico, Trebelli, Demeric Lablache and Ilma de Merska, and, I think, Christine Nilsson, though I am not quite certain if she was the Margaret when *Faust* was performed. So far as I could gather from those who witnessed some of these operas they had never been represented with such completeness in the town. Some years later, in 1877, another company from Her Majesty's Opera, under Mr Mapleson, came for a week. Madame Marie Roze, Madame de Belloca, Mdlle. Mila Rodani, Mdlle. Bauermeister, and Alwina Valeria were in the cast of *Un Ballo in Maschera*, *Il Trovatore*, *Marta*, *Faust*, and *Les Huguenots*; but the financial result was far from satisfactory. Equally unhappy was another Italian opera venture, when a most efficient company, with a continental reputation, visited us . . . The expenses . . . were so great . . . it would have been impossible to maintain the normal prices for seats . . . people hesitated before paying half a guinea for a place in the dress circle.

It was in 1881 that the reorganised Carl Rosa Company began their annual visits to Belfast, which were amazingly successful. The vocalists were mostly English and the ensemble showed a care and a completeness that had always been lacking in the more pretentious Italian opera. Miss Julia Gaylord, Miss Georgina Burns, Miss Clara Perry, Miss Marian Burton, and Miss Fanny Moody were all admirable vocalists, and with Mr Barton M'Guckin, Mr Ben Davies, Mr Snazelle, and Leslie Crotty such operas as *Mignon*, *Faust*, *Romeo and Juliet* and *Carmen* were adequately represented. During the next ten years a surprising variety of operatic works were produced under the same direction.

The year 1876 must be accounted as one of the most memorable in the history of the Belfast theatre. I have already referred to the influence upon the stock system of the visit of the complete touring company with Irving's plays; and now we were privileged to witness the most popular comedy of the day, *Our Boys*, played by a touring company of undoubted ability, and every one talked in such a way about the innovation that it became apparent that the stock 'support' would not be tolerated much longer. *Our Boys* had achieved the longest run on record in London, and the provincial company was in many respects superior to that at the Vaudeville, and the theatre was crowded every night during the week. Then in the autumn the whole Lyceum Company with Henry Irving and Miss Isabel Bateman came to us with *Hamlet*, *The Bells*, and Wills's *Charles I*. Extra scenery and appointments made this visit a memorable one. It was thought a very daring thing to bring to a town where Barry Sullivan had held practically undisputed sway in what was termed the 'legitimate' drama, a young actor who might possibly be regarded as a rival. It was reported that the older man had complained of the effrontery of the younger in essaying 'Hamlet – a part, sir, which every one knows I had practically made my own'. Playgoers in Belfast were, however, ready to give a young actor a chance of showing what he could do, and young Irving showed what he could do. His success was immediate, though not to such an extent as to do more than loosen the 'hooks of steel' that bound 'Barry' to the hearts of so many. What ever might be thought of the new Hamlet as compared with the old, there could be no doubt that Barry could not handle the part of Mathias in *The Bells*,[175] or that of the King in Wills's play; so when Barry came at Christmas he was welcomed as enthusiastically as before, and when Irving returned in due course he filled the theatre.

But the enterprise of Mr Warden went still further than to achieve the Lyceum engagement, for in the autumn of 1875 Signor Salvini with a full company came for three performances of *Othello* and *Hamlet* in Italian. I do not think that many people were impressed by the latter, but beyond a doubt the Othello of the great Italian was the finest impersonation ever seen in Belfast. It seemed to me overwhelming in force, not merely in the interpretation of jealousy, but in the lighter moments of the action. The Oriental savour of the Moor's infatuation impressed me. Every look that was cast at Desdemona was saturated, so to speak, with a consciousness of triumph that made the vehemence of the suspicion of infidelity more than plausible.

During the next year we had so many complete companies engaged in the representation of London successes that the stock companies were being gradually disbanded . . . Wilson Barrett's company, with Miss Caroline Heath, came with Wills's *Jane Shore*, and an adaptation of Sardou's *Fernande*, and the next year brought Miss Genevieve Ward with her *Forget-me-not*. With regard to Wills's drama I may mention that had it not been for the encouragement given by its reception in Belfast it would not have been given the chance of the long run it achieved the next year in London. It had already been tried in London and had failed to attract. Wilson Barrett induced the lessee of the Princess's to give it another trial, and it was played for six months.

Among the most successful of the ventures that followed hard upon the abolition of the local stock was the Compton Comedy Company. It was in 1881 that Edward Compton got around him a little band for the provincial representation of Goldsmith and Sheridan, with a completeness of detail that was quickly appreciated and rewarded year by year by crowded houses. He married Miss Virginia Bateman, and their elder son is now Compton Mackenzie, the novelist, while the youngest daughter is Miss Fay Compton, the leading comedy actress of to-day.[176] With the mention of these names I think I must bring these desultory recollections to a close. I had Compton Mackenzie in my arms when he was a month old, and I rocked the cradle in which Fay Compton was declining to go asleep. My pleasantest memories are of their parents and their grandparents.

Notes

NOTES TO INTRODUCTION

1 The principal sources for Moore's biography, other than scattered references in his non-fiction works, are an obituary in the *Belfast Telegraph* (12 May 1931), p. 3 and an article by 'Old Fogey' [E. G. Robinson] in the *Northern Whig* (15 May 1931, p. 13), which provoked some correspondence.

2 Frank Frankfort Moore, *The Truth About Ulster* (London, 1914), p. 43.

3 Moore, *Truth About Ulster*, pp. 199–205; see also Bernard McGinn *Antichrist: Two Thousand Years of the Human Fascination with Evil* (New York, 2000), p. 246 which notes Baxter as exemplifying the imbecility of many nineteenth-century historicist millenarians.

4 Moore, *Truth about Ulster*, pp. 194–5.

5 Thomas MacKnight *Ulster As It Is, or Twenty-Eight Years' Experience as an Irish Editor*, 2 vols (London, 1896) – the reference to 'our infidel contemporary' is noted on p. 17. A few of Moore's anecdotes in the present text may have been borrowed from MacKnight.

6 Letter from J. C. Orr, *Northern Whig*, 16 May 1931, p. 8.

7 Moore, *Truth About Ulster*, pp. 26–8.

8 For a fuller discussion of *The Ulsterman* see Patrick Maume, 'Three Ulstermen of letters: the Unionism of Frank Frankfort Moore, Shan Bullock and St John Ervine' in Richard English and Graham Walker (eds), *Unionism in Modern Ireland* (London/Dublin, 1996), pp. 63–80.

9 Eileen Black, *Art in Belfast 1760–1888: Art Lovers or Philistines?* (Dublin, 2006), pp. 139, 141, 155.

10 Ibid. This edition is heavily indebted to this useful work.

IN BELFAST BY THE SEA

1   A photograph of this fountain (by the locally based sculptor Giacomo Nannetti) is reproduced in Eileen Black, *Art in Belfast 1760–1888: Art Lovers or Philistines?* (Dublin, 2006), p. 108. The 'Crystal Palace' was destroyed by fire in 1864.

2   Eileen Black, *The People's Park: The Queen's Island, Belfast 1849–1879* (Belfast, 1988), is a brief history.

3   Moore probably means the Australian mining town (i.e. a hive of industry) rather than the American peak.

4   A reference to the post-war financial problems which led to the 1928 bankruptcy of the firm and its final disappearance in 1935. The debenture holders' claims would only be met after those of the preferred creditors, and were not secured by fixed assets; the joke implies their prospects of retrieving their capital are skeletal.

5   Samuel Smiles (1812–1904), author of numerous business biographies illustrating the message of hard work and foresight in his *Self-Help* (1859). 'Two of [his] sons, . . . were in business in Belfast, and when I went to live in London, my house was only half-a-dozen doors away from his residence. The old gentleman was as straight as his books at the age of eighty' (Frank Frankfort Moore, *The Truth About Ulster* (London, 1914), p. 163).

6   The hero-narrator of Coleridge's poem *The Ancient Mariner* incurs a curse by killing an albatross.

7   H. M. Pollock (1852–1937), Bangor-born businessman and educationalist; finance minister of Northern Ireland 1921–37. (*Oxford DNB* 'Hugh McDowell Pollock').

8   Frederick Marryat (1792–1848) author of popular naval novels and adventure stories for children.

9   A line from the popular hymn 'From Greenland's Icy Mountains' by Reginald Heber (1783–1826).

10   A jocular reference to Dickens's *Dombey and Son* (1846–8); the dying question of the boy Paul Dombey, 'What are the wild waves saying?' was a classic expression of Victorian sentimentality, from which the sardonic Moore distances himself.

11   Eugene Rimmel (1820–87) was a famous London-based perfumer (*Oxford DNB*). After harvesting, flax was rotted in water-filled hollows to extract the tough fibres from which linen is manufactured, producing a distinctive stench.

12   George Chadwick, Vicar of Belfast and later Bishop of Derry (*Truth About Ulster*, p. 209); Tresham Dames Gregg (1800–81) was a well-known Evangelical

Church of Ireland clergyman, populist preacher and anti-Catholic contro-versialist with strongly-held millenarian views (*Oxford DNB*).

13 For further information on Stewart (1825–94) see his *Oxford DNB* entry.

14 Like many Protestant observers, Moore thought Irish Catholic poverty partly due to abstaining from work on saints' festivals (*Truth About Ulster*, pp. 181–3).

15 Father of Rev. J. O. Hannay, well known as a humorous novelist under the pen-name 'George A. Birmingham'.

16 *Truth About Ulster*, pp. 218–20 has some further material about Rev. Beattie.

17 In Rhode Island; a major yachting centre. The Keys are a string of islands off the tip of Florida.

18 See W. S. Dale ,'Arthur David McCormick, R.I., Book Illustrator and Artist', *Irish Book Lover* 1 (August 1972), pp. 243–8. McCormick was born in Coleraine in 1860 and died in Dublin in 1943; in 1927 he redesigned the sailor's head emblem used by the cigarette company John Player & Sons, which still owned several of his maritime paintings in the early 1970s. This article includes a list of books illustrated by him.

19 In Kingstown/Dun Laoghaire.

20 Frederick Temple Hamilton-Temple Blackwood, first Marquess of Dufferin and Ava (1826–1902) North Down landowner and descendant of Richard Brinsley Sheridan; junior minister in Liberal governments 1864–6, 1868–72; governor-general of Canada 1872–8, ambassador to St Petersburg 1878–81, to Constan-tinople 1881–2; after reporting on Egyptian situation viceroy of India 1884–8, overseeing annexation of Burma; ambassador to Italy 1889–92, to France 1892–6. *Letters from High Latitudes* (published in 1856, an account of an 1854 voyage to Iceland and the Arctic) remains a recognised travel classic. (*Oxford DNB*)

21 Helen's Tower is a monument erected by Dufferin to his mother between Bangor and Newtownards.

22 The first Belfast shipyard was established in 1791 by William Ritchie from Ayrshire (b. 1760) and his brother Hugh (d. 1807) who opened a second shipyard in 1798, later inherited by his brother John (1751–1828) and then by John's son-in-law Alexander McLaine. These sites were displaced by William Dargan's new channel in the early 1840s; John Ritchie's former yard retained some access to the harbour while William's was filled in as a site for the Harbour Commissioner's office, so Moore's reference is presumably to the former (Michael Moss and John R. Hume *Shipbuilders to the World: 125 Years of Harland and Wolff, Belfast 1861–1986* (Belfast, 1986), pp. 1–10). The *Queen of the East* was not built by the business which became Harland & Wolff; presumably it was the work of a small local competitor.

23 Moore, *Truth About Ulster*, pp. 92–3 describes this meeting with slightly different emphases.

24 The developing area around St Malachy's Catholic Church in the Upper Markets area of South Belfast witnessed frequent sectarian disturbances in the mid-nineteenth century. See also Moore, *Truth About Ulster* p. 16.

25 Francis Charles Seymour-Conway, third Marquess of Hertford (1777–1842) owned extensive estates around Lisburn; he was an absentee landlord renowned for collecting art and loose women in his European travels, and was the model for the wealthy, dissolute Marquess of Steyne, who enters into compromising relations with Becky Sharpe in Thackeray's novel *Vanity Fair* (1848). He was not the father but the grandfather of the art collector and Lisburn MP (1873–85) Sir Richard Wallace (1818–90), non-marital son of Richard Seymour-Conway (1800–70), fourth Marquess of Hertford, who bequeathed his Lisburn estates to Wallace while the title passed to a distant cousin. Wallace's widow founded a London art museum, the Wallace Collection, in his memory. For the role of the Stannus family in managing the estate see Thomas MacKnight *Ulster As It Is, or Twenty-Eight Years' Experience as an Irish Editor*, 2 vols (London, 1896), I, pp. 202–3.

26 Prominent Evangelical clergyman (1835–1910), an interdenominational evangelist with strong links to the Brethren and an interest in Biblical prophecy (*Oxford DNB*). The Book of Daniel, with its portrayal of a ten-horned beast from the sea, a tyrannical 'king of the north' and a final apocalyptic persecution lasting 'a time, times, and a half' is a major source of Christian speculation on Antichrist and the Last Days (Paul Boyer, *When Time Shall Be No More: Prophecy Belief in Modern American Culture* (Cambridge MA, 1992), especially pp. 26–32). In *Truth About Ulster*, pp. 198–205. Moore has some kindly reminiscences of Guinness and bitter comments about the tendency of prophecy believers to treat 'the splendid and vivid imagery of one of the greatest of the Hebrew poets' as 'a jig-saw puzzle . . . [so that as a boy I] regretted exceedingly that the lions of King Darius had exercised so much self-restraint when they had the chance of a meal'.

27 E. S. W. de Cobain, an Orange populist; Unionist MP for East Belfast, 1885–92, expelled from the Commons for fleeing the country after being charged with homosexual offences; returned to Belfast and served a prison sentence. Moore called him 'a pretentious and sententious rascal . . . with a small fortune made by illicit means while in the employment of the Corporation' (Moore, *Truth about Ulster*, p. 247).

28 In the Book of Samuel David seeks refuge from Saul in the Cave of Adullam, where he gathers a band of outlaws, malcontents and masterless men; this

also refers to conservative Liberal MPs who brought down the Liberal Government in 1866 by siding with the Conservatives to oppose a Reform Bill.

29 *The Scapegoat* (1854) depicts the goat driven into the wilderness to atone for the sins of Israel (as specified in the Book of Leviticus) wandering on the desolate shore of the Dead Sea.

30 The second Marquess of Donegall was obliged to live in Belfast by heavy debts; legal difficulties and extravagance led to an 1822 settlement of the Donegall estate which (by granting long leases at nominal rents in return for immediate downpayments) contributed significantly to the development of nineteenth-century Belfast. From 1807 the Donegalls lived at Ormeau Cottage in Ballynafeigh (East Belfast); the inflow of cash after the 1822 settlement led to its extension in mock-Tudor style as 'Ormeau House'. After the Marquess's death in 1844 his successor lived in England. The house was rented out until 1857, when the contents were sold off and it was left derelict. The remains of the house were demolished after Belfast Corporation acquired the demesne as a public park in 1869.

31 This hothouse is still operational (2007) and stands in the Botanic Gardens near the Ulster Museum. It is known as the 'Tropical Ravine' and its flora include a banana tree. Eileen McCracken, 'Some nineteenth-century horticul-turalists', *Irish Booklore* 1: 2 (August 1972), pp. 179–83 includes a brief note on Charles M'Kimm (d. 1907). See also Eileen M'Cracken, *The Palm House and Botanic Garden, Belfast* (Belfast: Ulster Architectural Heritage Society, 1971).

32 29 June 1859.

33 The shop-looting described by Moore took place on 15 August 1864 as part of a series of riots sparked off by the burning of Daniel O'Connell in effigy as Catholic excursionists returned from the laying of the foundation stone for the O'Connell statue in Dublin. Some observers (including Moore) attribute the riots to the strengthening of the Catholic party by navvies working on a new dock. Jonathan Bardon, *Belfast: An Illustrated History* (Belfast, 1982), pp. 111–16; Moore, *Truth About Ulster*, pp. 15–32.

34 For a brief history of the Belfast police force see Brian Griffin, *The Bulkies: Police and Crime in Belfast 1800–1865* (Dublin, 1998).

35 The CSS *Alabama*, captained by Raphael Semmes, was a commerce raider built at Birkenhead in 1862 for the Confederate States Navy, which inflicted extensive damage on United States shipping before being sunk in August 1874. Public opinion in the Northern States was greatly antagonised by British willingness to build and embark this ship, and in 1871 an international tribunal awarded $15.5 m. compensation to the USA for damage inflicted by British-built commerce raiders.

36 Dolly Varden is a flirtatious young woman in Charles Dickens' *Barnaby Rudge* (1841); she gave her name to a type of flowered bonnet and a purple-and green muslin dress.

37 Belfast City Hall (of Portland stone and Italian marble) was built on the site of the former White Linenhall in Donegall Square; work began in 1896 and the building was completed in 1906.

38 See *Oxford DNB* on Sir Eyre Massey Shaw; he headed the Belfast police and fire services 1860-1, and lost both legs (not one as stated by Moore) in 1898. In the Gilbert and Sullivan opera *Iolanthe* (1182) the lovesick Fairy Queen invokes Captain Shaw, speculating 'Could thy brigade with cold cascade/ Quench my poor heart, I wonder'.

39 Lappers print patterns on linen.

40 The Bankruptcy Court.

41 For the role of Hugh C. Clarke (established as an auctioneer 1849) as dealer in fine art see Black, *Art in Belfast 1760-1888*, pp. 109, 136-7, 158-60. The exhibition referred to by Moore may have been one of the four large and well-advertised auctions mounted by Clarke on behalf of the Southport art dealer George Wilson between 1881 and 1886. (The 1881 sale included the first Whistler seen in Belfast.)

42 An account of the development of the pneumatic tyre and of this first race meeting, as told to the author by Dunlop, appears in Matthias M'Donnell Bodkin, *Recollections of an Irish Judge* (London, 1914), pp. 258-63; this, however, fails to mention Moore's point that the triumph of this first Dunlop bicycle was assisted by wet weather on the day of the meeting.

43 In Dickens's *Pickwick Papers* (1837)

44 A stone circle south of Belfast.

45 From 1891 the Belfast Water Commissioners developed a scheme to supply the city with water from the Mourne Mountains in South Down. The first stage was completed in 1901. After delays caused by the First World War, work on the great Silent Valley reservoir began in 1923 (as Moore was writing) and was completed in 1933. (Jack Loudan, *In Search of Water* (Belfast, 1940)).

46 Editor of *Illustrated London News*, 1891-1900, the *Sphere*, 1900-26. Married the Irish poet Dora Sigerson Shorter (1866-1918).

47 Black, *Art in Belfast 1760-1888*, p. 77 reproduces a prize waistcoat design made by John G. McGee & Co. for the 1851 Great Exhibition.

48 Robert Lloyd Praeger (1865-1953), naturalist who made many additions to the recognised flora and fauna of Ireland; best known to the general public for his account of Irish topography combined with recollections of field trips *The Way That I Went* (1937). For a brief account of the Patterson family see

J. R. R. Adams, 'From *Green Gravel* to *The Way that I Went*: folklife, literature and the Patterson family of Hollywood', *Linenhall Review* 10: 2 (winter 1993), pp. 4–7. *The Birds, Fishes and Cetacea of Belfast Lough*, mentioned by Moore, was actually written by Praeger's uncle Robert Lloyd Patterson (1836–1906).

49 For the printselling business of James Magill & Co (established 1848 and surviving to *c.*1899) see Black, *Art in Belfast 1760–1888*, pp. 116–19, 131–5, 150–1.

50 Marcus Ward & Co. was founded in 1836 by Marcus Ward, a paper manufacturer who shifted his firm's interest to printing and publishing, taking a pioneering interest in the use of colour lithography. After Ward's death in 1847 his sons Francis, William and John combined high technical and artistic standards to make the firm one of Britain's leading printers. The firm was particularly renowned for illuminated addresses, illustrated children's' books, greeting cards and the Vere Foster copybooks, which sold four million copies from 1865. Its demise was caused by failure to keep up with technological advances in photographic illustrations, as well as by the personal disputes described by Moore. http://www.belb.org.uk/libraries/libraries_marcus_ward.asp?ddid=3 (accessed 21 March 2006); Roger Dixon, *Marcus Ward & Co. of Belfast* (Belfast, 2004); Black, *Art in Belfast 1760–1888*.

51 Ward's held an exhibition of Wood's sculpture in 1870 Black, *Art in Belfast 1760–1888* p. 143. Wood (1827–86) was born in Manchester and trained in London and Edinburgh before settling in Rome from the late 1850s; he developed an Ulster clientele and visited the province in 1870. The Ulster Museum (Belfast) holds some of his pieces.

52 For Vinycomb's role in the late Victorian Belfast art scene see Black, *Art in Belfast 1760–1888*, pp. 151–2, 173–4, 186.

53 Kate (Catherine) Greenaway (1846–1901) one of the most famous Victorian illustrators of children's books, known for dream-like imagery of fairies and young girls. Her connection with Ward's in her early career ended in 1877 after they refused to publish verses she composed to accompany her drawings and reproduced some of her images without permission (*Oxford DNB*).

54 See Black, *Art in Belfast 1760–1888*, pp. 198–9, 207. City status was conferred in 1888.

55 Margaret MacNeill, *Vere Foster, An Irish Benefactor* (Belfast, 1971).

56 Sir Edward Poynter (1826–1919), Victorian painter: Director of the National Gallery 1894–1904, President of the Royal Academy, 1896–1918.

57 Moore's account should be supplemented by reference to Diane Gracey, 'The Decline and Fall of Marcus Ward', *Irish Booklore* 1: 2 (August 1972), pp. 186–202, which draws on archives of Brett & Co, the solicitors employed by John Ward and Vere Foster. The dispute arose because Foster, whose business

arrangement with John Ward was informal, allowed the firm to continue printing his exercise books for a period after the resignation of John Ward in 1876 in order to defray their financial obligations to the former partner. Foster meant this as a temporary concession; he believed his agreement with John Ward had been personal and that he was entitled to transfer his business away from the firm of Marcus Ward whenever John Ward found himself able to take it on (which he did after two years by entering into an agreement with Blackie's, an Edinburgh-based printing firm). The directors of Marcus Ward & Co., on the other hand, believed Foster's original agreement had been with the firm rather than John Ward personally, and that his decision to allow the firm to continue printing the books after John Ward's departure amounted to a commitment to remain with them indefinitely; they had made considerable investment based on this assumption. Brett & Co. believed much of the blame for the dispute lay with the new manager-partner, William Yeates [whose name Moore, writing from memory, misspells] whom they considered had deliberately sowed dissension between the Ward brothers; Gracey suspects, however, that to some extent John Ward used Foster as a catspaw in his dispute with the firm, since the philanthropist was better-placed to attract sympathy than the hard-headed businessman. This suspicion underlies Moore's final contrast between Foster's self-imposed poverty and the comfortable lifestyle enjoyed by John Ward.

58 The Belfast Free Library was opened on 13 October 1888; the exhibition mentioned by Moore ran from 17 October to 1 December 1888 and led to the opening of Belfast's first public art gallery in 1890. For a description see Black, *Art in Belfast 1760–1888*, pp. 208–10.

59 George C. Hyndman's auctioneering firm operated 1807–66 and was the dominant auctioneering firm in early Victorian Belfast (Black, *Art in Belfast*, pp. 39, 54–6, 135–7).

60 The upas tree allegedly poisoned all living things around it; in 1868 Gladstone used it as a metaphor for the established status of the Church of Ireland.

61 Now Ghana; 'Factories' = trading-posts.

62 John Cramsie founded his auctioneering business in 1846 and it long survived his death in 1881; in the 1860s he was Belfast's foremost auctioneer of fine art. Black, *Art in Belfast*, pp. 109–10, 135–8, 158.

63 Hamilton's firm was founded in 1863, in the 1860s it was the most active after Cramsie, holding a number of fine-art auctions as well as his main line of work – auctions derived from house clearances (Black, *Art in Belfast 1760–1888*, pp. 135–6). Salvator Rosa (1615–73) Neapolitan baroque painter

known for paintings of wild, picturesque landscapes, very popular in the early nineteenth century; Rosa Bonheur (1822–99) French realist painter specialising in pictures of animals. If Moore's account is credible, Hamilton's mistake may be partly due to the fact that Magill's had held a widely publicised and prestigious exhibition of Bonheur's painting, *The Horse Fair*, in 1859 (Black, pp. 118–19).

64 Belfast publishers, best remembered for their Parlour Library (from 1846) which pioneered the production of cheap 'yellowback' one-volume reprints of popular novals. Irish publishers of several novels by William Carleton.

65 James Sheridan Knowles (1784–1862) lived and taught in Belfast 1810–17, where he wrote and staged his plays *Brian Boromhe* (1810) and *Caius Gracchus* (1815). He taught for a time at the Royal Belfast Academical Institution, later Moore's *alma mater*.

66 Authors of adventure stories very popular with boys, and prohibited by Moore's father. ('Novels were shut out from us – even the stirring, healthy romances of W. H. G. Kingston and R. M. Ballantyne were prohibited – but there was not a boy's bed that did not hold between the mattress and its foundation a copy of *The White Chief*, *The Scalp Hunters* or *The Rifle Rangers*', Moore, *Truth About Ulster*, pp. 165–6).

67 John Edward Jenkins (1838–1910) satirical and social reform novelist; his immensely popular *Ginx's Baby* (1870) describes wasteful and futile struggles between rival religious agencies for possession of a navvy's thirteenth child. (*Oxford DNB*; John Sutherland *Longman Companion to Victorian Fiction* (London, 1988), pp. 246–7, 330–1.) *Lutchmee and Dilloo* has attracted some attention as 'the earliest novel of Indo-Guyanese life' and was reprinted in Macmillan's Caribbean Classics series in 2003.

68 For Rodman's role in the Belfast art trade see Black, *Art in Belfast*, pp. 143–50; he had held exhibitions from 1872 but opened his purpose-built art gallery in October 1877; his annual 'black and white exhibitions' (from 1879) were one of the events of the year in local art circles (ibid., pp. 145–6; the *Newsletter* comment quoted on p. 146 may be by Moore.)

69 For the popularity of the historical and religious paintings of Sir Joseph Noel Paton (1821–1901) in nineteenth-century Belfast, see Black, *Art in Belfast*, pp. 147–50; ten of his paintings were displayed in Belfast single-picture shows between 1864 and 1888. *Mors Janua Vitae* (Death the Gateway to Life) was painted by him in 1866. *Hercules Wrestling with Death for the Body of Alcestis* (1869–71) is by Frederic Leighton (1830–96). Black mentions two paintings by the leading pre-Raphaelite Holman Hunt being exhibited in Belfast (*The Finding of the Saviour in the Temple* in 1865; *The Shadow of Death*

in 1875); Hunt's *The Light of the World* (1851–3) was immensely popular and widely reproduced.

70 The Belfast Ramblers' Sketching Club was founded 1879 by John Vinycomb and 16 members of Wards' staff; they reorganised in 1885, became the Belfast Art Society (1890–1930), then the Ulster Academy of Arts (1930–1950), and finally the Royal Ulster Academy (1950–) – Black, *Art in Belfast*, pp. 151–3.

71 For Magill's photography business (from 1861) see Black *Art in Belfast 1760–1888* p. 135.

72 Founder of the better-known Jury's Hotel in Dublin; the name survives to the present day as the title of an Irish hotel group.

73 Later King Edward VII.

74 John Tyndall (1820–93), physicist and advocate of scientific naturalism, from a Carlow Protestant family. His Belfast speech declared science would produce a comprehensive account of the universe without reference to supernatural causes. See also *Truth About Ulster*, pp. 221–6, which contrasts the outcry with the subsequent enthusiasm for an anti-Home Rule speech delivered by Tyndall in Belfast in 1890 (for which see also MacKnight, *Ulster As It Is*, II, pp. 252–3). Columbariums are dovecotes. See also John Wilson Foster, *Recoveries* (Dublin, 2002) and David Livingstone, 'Darwin in Belfast: The Evolution Debate', in John Wilson Foster (ed.), *Nature in Ireland: A Scientific and Cultural History* (Dublin, 1997), pp. 387–408.

75 Derryvolgie Avenue, off the Malone Road in South Belfast, then a wealthy residential area.

76 See also Patrick Maume (ed.), William McComb, *The Repealer Repulsed* (Dublin, 2003) and Patrick Maume 'From Scotia's Storied Land: William McComb and Ulster-Scottish Presbyterian Identity' forthcoming in James McConnell and Frank Ferguson (eds), *Across the Water: Nineteenth-Century Ireland and Scotland* (Dublin: 2007). Black, *Art in Belfast 1760–1888*, p. 60 has some information on McComb's printselling activities.

77 For the career of the painter Thomas Robinson (d. 1810) and his *Review of the Belfast Yeomanry* see Black, *Art in Belfast 1760–1888*, pp. 6–10. *Juvenile Poems* appeared in 1806.

78 The Social Science Congress in fact took place in 1867; the clash between Dufferin and Bateson is described in MacKnight, *Ulster As It Is*, I, pp. 111–14 which may be Moore's ultimate source here.

79 William Thomson (1824–1907), the major physicist of late Victorian Britain, was born in Belfast, though his family moved to Glasgow in 1832. See *Oxford DNB*.

80 The *Oxford DNB* has an entry on John Perry (1850–1920).

81 *Oxford DNB* has entry on Sir Charles Wyville Thomson (1830–82). A Scot, he was professor of mineralogy and geology at QCB 1854–70 (adding the professorship of natural history in 1862; he moved to the chair of natural history at Edinburgh in 1870. The *Challenger* expedition (1872–6) was the first attempt to carry out a systematic survey of the depths of the world's oceans; it inaugurated modern oceanography.

82 *Oxford DNB* entry on Sir Joseph Larmor (1857–1942): Larmor combined his work as a Cambridge-based physicist with strong Unionist political commitments (he was Unionist MP for Cambridge University 1911–22) and returned to Ulster on his retirement in 1932.

83 The organ installed by Rev. Robert Workman in his suburban Newtonbreda church produced intense controversy, as it disregarded the previous Presbyterian prohibition on instrumental music; part of the general assembly waged a long and unsuccessful campaign to suppress it (Margaret Garner, *Robert Workman of Newtonbreda* (Belfast, 1969)).

84 There is an *Oxford DNB* entry on Hugh Thomson (1860–1920).

85 The self-taught Richard Hooke (1820–1908) came from Belfast and was the town's most prominent portrait painter, 1843–57; he visited it every January and February in search of commissions after settling in Manchester in 1857. His practice of painting from photographs dates from 1856. (Black, *Art in Belfast 1760–1888*, pp. 52–4, 105.) Since Hooke remained in contact with Belfast's artistic circles it is a sign of Moore's disdain that he did not know – or care – about Hooke's Belfast origins.

86 For Jones's growing connection with Belfast from the mid-1870s and his public rivalry with Hooke over Corporation commissions in the early 1880s see Black, *Art in Belfast 1750–1888*, pp. 147, 152–3, 196–8.

87 The Liberal Lord Chancellor Lord Haldane was driven from office in 1915 after a vitriolic journalistic campaign, which cited a pre-war speech (at a German academic gathering) where he described Germany as his 'spiritual home' to convey admiration for the German philosophical tradition. Moore thus makes a veiled insinuation of treasonable behaviour against Lavery.

88 This was organised by Lady Gregory (Lane's aunt) late in 1916 after the London National Gallery refused to give effect to the wish expressed in an unwitnessed (therefore not legally binding) codicil that his Impressionist pictures should go to Dublin rather than to London as stated in his earlier, legally valid, will.

89 During the 1916 Easter Rising.

90 Anthony Carey Stannus was a distinguished pupil of the Belfast School of Design in 1852 and taught at Dowlais in Wales before becoming a leading

figure in the late Victorian Belfast art scene; his works frequently appeared in local exhibitions. He was elected president of the Belfast Ramblers' Sketching Club in 1866 and served on the board of the Belfast school of Art 1889–94 (Black, *Art in Belfast 1760–1888*).

91 For Margaret Byers (*née* Morrow), founder of Victoria College, Belfast, see her *Oxford DNB* entry and Alison Jordan, *Margaret Byers: Pioneer of Women's Education* (Belfast, 1987). Sir John Byers (1853–1920) was professor of midwifery at Queen's University, Belfast.

92 Sir William Whitla (1855–1933), physician and diagnostician, professor of materia medica at Queen's University Belfast and Unionist MP for the university 1918–23, as well as physician to the Royal Victoria Hospital. His books on *Elements of Pharmacy* (1882) and *A Dictionary of Treatment* (1892) were bestsellers; much of the wealth gained from them was donated to Queen's University Belfast, whose Whitla Hall is called after him. The stained-glass window mentioned by Moore shows the Good Samaritan and commemorates the bravery of two Ulster doctors during an epidemic. (*Oxford DNB*)

93 English neoclassical artist (1755–1834).

94 MacKnight *Ulster As It Is*, I, p. 238 states that the refusal of Dr Murney (whom MacKnight does not name) to abandon Freemasonry led Bishop Dorrian of Down and Connor to display hostility not only to the doctor but to his entire family. (Dr Murney's father had been a prominent Belfast merchant.)

95 John Abernethy (1764–1831) famous London surgeon.

96 Moore gives a different account of this sermon in *Truth About Ulster* (p. 206), stating the subject was the identity of Rome with the Babylon of the Apocalypse. He remarks on Cooke's distinguished appearance, and notes that 'In his day he was . . . a fine preacher though, of course, there were people who called him rabid . . . the pamphlet [*The Repealer Repulsed*] which was published by his authority and was supposed to embody the eloquence that had swept the most brilliant debater in the Kingdom off the platform, made me feel that if the Presbyterian champion was able to accomplish his purpose by such an effort as that which was attributed to him, the Irish Liberator must have been in a singularly yielding mood.'

97 James Morgan (1799–1873), minister of Fisherwick Place, Belfast from 1828. Closely allied with Henry Cooke in the Subscription Controversy, heavily involved in philanthropic work (including missions to the urban poor and to overseas non-Christians); moderator of the general assembly 1846. His son edited his autobiography for posthumous publication (1874).

98 John Edgar (1798–1866) celebrated for advocacy of teetotalism and missions to Irish Catholics (*The Cry from Connaught* (1846)).

99 For Toye's (1801–70) career see *Brief Memorials of the Late Rev. Thomas Toye, Belfast by his Widow* (Belfast, 1873) – for his populist style and metaphors see pp194–5. The story about his smoking in the pulpit arose because he smoked a pipe full of tobacco mixed with stranmonium to gain relief from asthma (p. 99). He played a major role in the spread of the 1859 Ulster Revival to Belfast from its north Antrim origins; since hearing of the American revival of 1858 he had prayed for its appearance in Ulster and he brought lay-preachers from Ahoghill to Belfast in May 1859 to describe their experiences (pp. 55–6). In his anti-Revival work *The Year of Delusion* (Belfast, 1860), Rev. Isaac Nelson claims Rev. William Gibson's official history of the Revival, *The Year of Grace*, suppresses Toye's role for fear the Revival might be discredited by association with his eccentricity. Rev. Ian Paisley describes Toye ('the outstanding soul-winning minister in Belfast') as one of his role models.

100 *Truth About Ulster*, pp. 188–97 has a much more sardonic account of the Revival which compares the participants to West Indian negroes reduced to hysteria by religious camp-meetings, refers to sexual immorality among converts and preachers, and mocks the evangelists' self-righteous assurance that they were saved and most others damned.

101 Dwight Lyman Moody (1837–99) and Ira David Sankey (1840–1909) were American evangelists who adapted the old-style revival meeting to a genteel middle-class audience; Moody preached and Sankey sang hymns to his own harmonium accompaniment. Their visit to Belfast took place in 1874 during a two-year tour of the British Isles (*Oxford DNB*). Moore gives a more detailed and sardonic account of their visit in *Truth About Ulster*, pp. 226–9.

102 *Fra Diavolo* (Brother Satan) is an 1830 opera by the French composer Daniel Auber about a Neapolitan ex-monk turned bandit.

103 The Anacreontic Society already existed in 1829, when the Belfast Savings Bank in May Street incorporated a large upstairs music room for its meetings (Bardon, *Belfast*, p. 75). It was called after the Greek poet Anacreon who celebrated wine, women and song. For the building of the Music Hall to accommodate it (1840) see Black, *Art in Belfast 1760–1888*, pp. 30, 46–7.

104 Edmund Kean (1787–1833) and his son Charles (1811–68) were celebrated Shakespearean actors.

105 By Handel; based on the tragedy by Racine.

106 *Preciosa* (1811) is a play by the German dramatist Pius Alexander Wolff, for which Carl Maria von Weber (1786–1826; best remembered for his 1821 opera *Der Freischutz*) composed incidental music in 1820.

107   Swedish opera singer (1820–87).

108   The midget Charles Sherwood Stratten (1838–83) achieved celebrity by touring as 'General Tom Thumb' under the management of the showman P. T. Barnum (1810–91).

109   John Nevil Maskelyne (1839–1917) celebrated Victorian conjuror.

110   In the Biblical *First Book of Samuel* (chapter 28), the disintegrating King Saul employs a witch, living at a place called Endor, to consult the spirit of the prophet Samuel, who foretells his defeat by the Philistines and death.

111   Pepper's Ghost is a theatrical illusion which uses mirrors and lighting effects to create the illusion of a transparent onstage ghost. 'Zazel' may be another name for the chess-playing pseudo-automata 'Ajeeb' (1868–1929, which had a chessplayer concealed inside it) or 'Mephisto' (1876–7), operated at a distance by electro-magnetic means.

112   Dion Boucicault (1820–90) celebrated Irish-born author of melodramas.

113   Edward Saunderson, Cavan landlord, Liberal MP for Cavan 1865–74, Conservative MP for North Armagh and Ulster Unionist leader 1885–1906. He loved to act the stage-Irishman in order to gratify his sense of humour and present all Irishmen including himself as quaint creatures unfit for self-government; a favourite tactic was to make provocative statements, hoping Nationalist MPs would make themselves ridiculous by losing their tempers. Reginald Lucas *Colonel Saunderson MP* (London, 1908); Alvin Jackson *Colonel Edward Saunderson: Land and Loyalty in Victorian Ireland* (1995); Patrick Maume 'Music-Hall Unionism: Robert Martin and the Politics of the Stage-Irishman' in Peter Gray (ed.), *Victoria's Ireland? Irishness and Britishness, 1837–1901* (Dublin, 2004), pp. 69–80.

114   Edmund Thomas Chipp (1823–86), Ulster Hall organist and conductor to various Belfast musical societies 1862–6; organist and master of choristers at Ely Cathedral, 1866–86. (*Oxford DNB*).

115   According to the *Oxford DNB* entry for Alfred Cellier (1844–91) he left Belfast in 1898 to become organist at St Alban's Holborn. This entry makes clear, as Moore does not, that 'Queen of My Heart' was composed by Cellier.

116   Richard D'Oyly Carte (1844–91) the impresario who produced Gilbert and Sullivan's Savoy Operas.

117   East Kent Regiment.

118   Blown down by trumpets (Book of Joshua).

119   This version of the Bateman–Irving breach contrasts with Robertson Davies's *Oxford DNB* entry on Sir Henry Irving, which states 'The best evidence shows that it was achieved with goodwill on both sides and a realistic acceptance by Mrs Bateman' while noting the claim by Compton Mackenzie

(Mrs Bateman's grandson) that there was considerable bitterness on both sides. Moore's first-hand account, coming from a witness in touch with the Irving circle through Bram Stoker, strongly supports the Mackenzie version.

120 1831 narrative poem by Thomas Hood (1799–1845), largely spoken by the anti-hero who describes (supposedly from imagination, actually from experience) the torments of guilt which pursue a murderer.

121 Oratorio by Handel; this bass duet celebrates the overthrow of Pharaoh's army in the Red Sea.

122 Allan James Foli (1825–89) came from Cahir, Co. Tipperary (*Oxford DNB*).

123 1826 opera by Carl Maria von Weber.

124 Mikhail Glinka's *A Life for the Tsar* (1836) depicts the self-sacrifice of Ivan Susanin, who offers to guide Polish troops pursuing Mikhail Romanov (founder of the Russian imperial dynasty) and leads them astray at the cost of his own life.

125 Mendelssohn's 1846 oratorio *Elijah* was immensely popular with nineteenth-century British audiences; its subject matter and the fact that it was given as a choral performance appealed to members of minority religious cultures suspicious of drama in general.

126 Sir Charles Santley (1834–1922) – see *Oxford DNB*.

127 Sir George Henschel (1850–1934), singer and conductor, first performed in England in 1877 after beginning his career in Germany

128 The Congress of Berlin (1878) was a conference of the Great Powers aimed at reorganising the Balkans after Russia's victory over Turkey in 1877–8; it reflected fears of Russian expansionism.

129 A cantata (1886) by Sir Arthur Sullivan, very popular with late Victorian choral groups.

130 The celebrated Carl Rosa Opera Company (called after its founding impresario, 1842–89) was founded in 1873 and toured Britain performing English-language versions of operas until 1958; the name was revived in 1988 for a touring light opera company.

131 The five grades of the knightly Order of St Gregory the Great are the highest pontifical honour available to laymen.

132 Also known as *La Muette de Portici* (1828).

133 Eugene Goossens *père* (1845–1906), Belgian-born conductor with the Carl Rosa opera company from 1873. His son and namesake (1867–1958) was a conductor and violinist: his grandson Sir Eugene Aynsley Goossens was a well-known conductor and composer, director of the Cincinnati and Sydney Symphony Orchestras.

134 John Chippindale Montesquieu Bellew (1823–74) was a popular London Anglican clergyman and preacher who became a public reader and reciter

after his conversion to Catholicism in 1868 (*Oxford DNB*). The unctuous preacher Charles Honeyman appears in *Thackeray's* novel *The Newcomes* (1853–5).

135 Frederick Samuel Boas (1862–1957), Fellow of Balliol College, Oxford. His works included *Shakespeare and His Predecessors* (1896) and *Songs of Ulster and Balliol* (1917).

136 William J. Lawrence (1862–1940), Belfast-born theatrical historian and drama critic, argued much can be gained in understanding Shakespeare by reconstructing the physical lay-out and conditions of the Elizabethan playhouse (Robert Welch (ed.), *The Oxford Companion to Irish Literature* (Oxford, 1996), pp. 302–3.)

137 This *Northern Star* appeared 1868–72; should not be confused with the United Irish paper of the 1790s or Joseph Devlin's paper of the late 1890s and early 1900s.

138 The *Belfast Morning News* was a Catholic daily paper founded in 1855. Taken over by the Gray family of the *Freeman's Journal*, it followed their lead in supporting Parnell at the time of the Split (1890); in 1891 the *Irish News* was founded with clerical support, and secured so much of the older paper's readership that the *Morning News* was forced to amalgamate with it in 1892.

139 Of Presbyterian and tenant-right sympathies; published 1842–69.

140 Charles Arthur Russell (1832–1900), born in Newry, practised as a solicitor in Belfast, July 1854–November 1856, where he subsequently became a barrister. Liberal MP for Louth 1880–5, for South Hackney 1885–94; Lord Chief Justice and first Lord Russell of Killowen, 1894–1900.

141 Although Moore's account of Rea as a self-publicising eccentric reflects the solicitor's later years (when Moore knew him) it underestimates his importance in his earlier career as a populist rabble-rouser veering between Orangeism and Fenianism. His major achievement was the exposure of dubious financial practices by Belfast Corporation through a June 1855 lawsuit which led to the downfall of Town Clerk and Belfast Conservative political boss John Bates (Ian Budge and Cornelius O'Leary, *Belfast: Approach to Crisis – A Study of Belfast Politics, 1613–1970* (London, 1970), pp. 60–5). This was followed by a long-running attempt to pass an Indemnity Act for the affected councillors on the grounds that much of the unauthorised expenditure had been beneficial to the town; parliamentary hearings were marked by clashes between Rea and Conservative witnesses, leading to such incidents as that mentioned by Moore. For another brief and hostile account of Rea see MacKnight *Ulster As It Is*, I, pp. 124–5.

142 Richard, Duke of Gloucester (later King Richard III) is the anti-hero of Shakespeare's *Richard III*, who regularly makes cynical comments to the

audience disclosing his various plots and schemes. In the first act he successfully woos Lady Anne Neville, whose husband he has just murdered. Shakespeare emphasises Richard's hunchback. (Biggar was also a hunchback.)

143 Joseph Gillies Biggar (1828–90) Home Rule MP for Cavan 1874–85, for Cavan West 1885–90. The Hyland case took place in March 1883; Biggar famously declared there was an impediment to marriage with Miss Hyland – two other women by whom he had children.

144 Hugh McCalmont Cairns (1819–85), Conservative MP for Belfast 1852–68, Lord Chancellor 1868, 1874–80; Conservative leader in the Lords 1868–70; distinguished advocate and jurist, significant adviser to Derby and Disraeli; outspokenly evangelical. (*Oxford DNB*).

145 Moore goes on to describe how Miss Finney, who appeared under the stage name May Fortescue, had a minor part in the Savoy Operas. The Cairns family, whose ultra-evangelicalism gave them a particularly strong disapproval of the theatre (Lady Cairns was a niece of the famous Antrim-born Evangelical clergyman Hugh M'Neile) pressurised Garmoyle into breaking the engagement. Miss Finney, supported by friends who included W. S. Gilbert and Angela Burdett-Coutts, issued a writ for breach of promise of marriage. The case was settled for £10,000. Moore's assertion that Cairns descended from a butler provoked an angry correspondence in the *Belfast Telegraph*; a correspondent, 'H. C. L.' established fairly clearly that the claim was unfounded (*Belfast Telegraph* 10, 20 June 1924). *Truth* was a satirical magazine run by the Liberal MP Henry Labouchere; it specialised in exposing scandals which other papers feared to touch, was frequently sued for libel, and might be described as a Victorian *Private Eye*.

146 Moore's scathing account of Cairns's relationship to Belfast (which was challenged by several letter-writers in the *Belfast Telegraph*) bears some resemblance to MacKnight *Ulster As It Is*, I, 72–9; it is possible that Moore draws on the older man's account.

147 Sir Thomas M'Clure (1806–93) Belfast merchant and property developer, leading figure of Ulster Liberalism; MP for Belfast 1868–74, for Co. Londonderry 1878–85; married Ellison Thorburn 1877. For a more favourable account see MacKnight, *Ulster As It Is*, I, pp. 159–61.

148 Moore's references are all to the 1868 election: the Orange-populist Johnston and the Liberal McClure, in informal alliance, defeated the official Conservatives Lanyon and Mulholland. MacKnight, who was central to the creation of this Liberal–Orange populist axis, describes the contest extensively in *Ulster as it is*.

149 Tupto, to punish/beat; tuptomai, I am punished/beaten (Greek).

150 Xenophon's *Anabasis*, describing the retreat to the Black Sea of an army of Greek mercenaries after their unsuccessful invasion of Persia; a basic text for learners of Greek.

151 In *Stalky and Co.* (1899)

152 1851 novel by the popular Ulster-born writer of Western adventures, Mayne Reid (1818–83); his other novels included *The Headless Horseman* (1866) for which see below. (*Oxford DNB*).

153 Martin Tupper (1810–89), immensely popular mid-Victorian author of platitudinous moral verse; Algernon Charles Swinburne (1837–1909) won fame and notoriety with poetry combining technical virtuosity with republicanism, hostility to Christianity, and sexual (often sado-masochistic) themes.

154 Tom Taylor (1817–80), popular Victorian playwright whose extensive borrowings from French drama led to accusations of plagiarism; wrote for *Punch* from 1844, editor 1874–80. (*Oxford DNB*).

155 See J. L. McCracken, *New Light at the Cape of Good Hope: William Porter, the Father of Cape Liberalism* (Belfast, 1993).

156 Andrew Porter (1837–1919), Liberal MP for Co. Londonderry 1880–3; solicitor-general for Ireland 1881, attorney-general for Ireland 1883, master of the rolls for Ireland 1883–1906 (*Oxford DNB*).

157 Lord Mayor of Belfast 1910–14, prominent campaigner against the Third Home Rule Bill; Unionist MP for East Belfast 1910–14. His statue outside Belfast City Hall (by F. W. Pomeroy) was unveiled in 1919.

158 James McCosh (1811–94), professor of logic and philosophy at Queen's College Belfast, 1851–68, president of Princeton, 1868–88.

159 Thomas Andrews (1813–85) vice-president of Queen's College Belfast, 1845–79, professor of chemistry 1849–79; made important discoveries on ozone, heat of combination and liquefaction of gases (*Oxford DNB*).

160 Moore, *The Truth About Ulster*, pp. 75–8.

161 Rev. James Owen Hannay (1865–1950) wrote many humorous plays and novels under the pseudonym 'George A. Birmingham'.

162 In R. B. Sheridan's *The Rivals*.

163 In Goldsmith's *She Stoops to Conquer*.

164 Edward O'Connor Terry (1844–1912) actor and theatre proprietor. His *Oxford DNB* entry notes he began in the early 1860s with 'minor roles in a series of provincial theatres'.

165 In 1871. The *Athenaeum* was a weekly review which published extensive surveys of developments in science and the arts.

166 1864 melodrama by Dion Boucicault (1820–90)

167 Gustavus Vaughan Brooke (1818–66) Dublin-born actor (*Oxford DNB*); the reference is to Cassio's drunkenness in *Othello* Act II, scene 3.

168 For Charles Dillon (1819–81) see *Oxford DNB*.

169 Mercerisation is a process in which cotton is given a lustrous silk-like finish and rendered more receptive to dye by being immersed in caustic soda, then neutralised; Moore suggests the style of drama he describes is a synthetic substitute for the real thing.

170 In the 1839 play *Richelieu, or the Conspiracy* by Edward Bulwer Lytton (1803–73).

171 In *Money* (1840) by Bulwer Lytton.

172 The generous, reckless brother and rival of the malevolent hypocrite Joseph Surface in Sheridan's play *The School for Scandal*.

173 Hero of Bulwer Lytton's play *The Lady of Lyons* (1838).

174 By Tom Taylor (1862). The comic aristocrat Lord Dundreary amused America; Abraham Lincoln was watching the play when assassinated.

175 Matthias in Leopold Lewis's *The Bells* (the role which made Irving's reputation) is an outwardly respectable citizen who founded his fortunes by robbing and murdering a pedlar, and disintegrates under his hidden guilt.

176 Compton Mackenzie (1883–1972) writer and flamboyant Scottish nationalist, now best remembered for such works as the humorous novel *Whiskey Galore*; Fay Compton (1894–1978) actress whose career was at its peak in the 1920s, best remembered for playing Ophelia and J. M. Barrie's Mary Rose (*Oxford DNB*).